Life

MAPPiNG

Life

MAPPiNG

Create a powerful blueprint to bring out
the best in your self – and your life

Brian and Sangeeta Mayne

Vermilion
LONDON

12

Published in 2002 by Vermilion
an imprint of Ebury Press, Random House, 20 Vauxhall Bridge Road, London SW1V 2SA
www.randomhouse.co.uk

Address for companies within The Random House Group Limited can be found at:
www.randomhouse.co.uk/office.htm

The Random House Group Limited Reg. No. 954009

Illustrations by Rob Loxston

The Random House Group Limited supports The Forest Stewardship
Council® (FSC®), the leading international forest-certification organisation.
Our books carrying the FSC label are printed on FSC®-certified paper.
FSC is the only forest-certification scheme supported by the leading
environmental organisations, including Greenpeace. Our
paper procurement policy can be found at
www.randomhouse.co.uk/environment

FSC
www.fsc.org
MIX
Paper from
responsible sources
FSC® C016897

A CIP catalogue record for this book is available from the British Library

ISBN 9780091884550

Printed and bound in Great Britain by Clays Ltd, St Ives plc

CONTENTS

We dedicate this book

to all the peoples of the Earth.

May its contents help you find

Enjoyment, Prosperity, Freedom and Love.

Acknowledgements

Countless people have given loving support over the years, and we express our deep gratitude to:

- Julia McCutchen, our editor, whose guidance, experience, understanding and patience have helped to create a smoother and clearer flow in the presentation of *Life Mapping*.
- all our family, friends and colleagues for their encouragement, love and belief in us.
- those who have attended our workshops and coaching sessions for sharing their openness, experiences and successes.

We bless and thank you all for your personal kindnesses and contributions.

PREFACE

In the recession of the early 1990s my business crashed dramatically and I lost everything – my livelihood, my home, most of my possessions – and my marriage fell apart. I faced a situation where not only had I lost the personal things that I counted as my life, but in addition I was just under £1 million in debt. Everything seemed bleak – I had no formal qualifications or work experience, I moved back with my parents and spent a year on charity – but the thing that scared me most was that at nearly thirty years of age I still couldn't read or write properly.

I now look back on all of this as an absolute blessing. The path that has unfolded since then has led me into an understanding of the mysteries and principles of success and, through their application, the creation of a new life, a fantastic second marriage to a wonderful new wife, a new home and, in just a few short weeks, the birth of our first child.

If there is one single thing that I could attribute this dramatic turn around in my fortunes to it is the development and practice of the technique I call Life Mapping. For me this book is a way of sharing with others a little of the freedom, power and joy that I have received in such abundance.

BRIAN MAYNE

Meeting Brian some years ago was such a blessing for me. I found not only my true life partner and teacher but also someone who shared the beliefs and values I had come to live my life by.

Having embarked on an incredible journey of self-discovery at the age of twenty-seven – sparked off by various life circumstances, mostly sorrowful ones – I had arrived at a place of what I knew to be fulfilment. I had a strong sense of purpose which carried with it an experience of trust, flow and peace that I had never known before. Seven years into my journey I met Brian, and I then finally felt ready to embrace the next part of my life.

By that time I had built up a very successful life-coaching and training practice based purely on my innermost desire to help people know The Gift of Self, for I felt that this was what I had been given – the opportunity to embrace the authentic gift of me. Through the use of finely developed tools that enable people to do this, the practice became popular with individuals from many different walks of life – from students to high-profile executives of blue-chip companies – all wanting to know their self and realize their true potential in life.

The next stage of my journey has been one of continuing evolution and grace. As I write this preface there are just two weeks to go before the arrival of our precious gift from the universe – our child. I have no doubt that this child within me decided to come into our lives at exactly the same time as the opportunity arose to write this book, so that he/she could also contribute. From start to finish it has taken us approximately nine months to put on to paper what we have been living, sharing and dancing over the last few years – Life Mapping.

I met Brian when Life Mapping was in its early stages of development, so I have had the opportunity to delve deeply into its potential. I have morphed it, played with it and applied it in every conceivable way until, finally, I have reached the point of knowing its awesome power as a tool for self-awareness, purpose, healing, and mapping one's gift. I can put my hand on my heart and say that Life Mapping has become one of my most favoured tools for coaching and training, and even now I still marvel at the outstanding results this simple yet profound system produces.

Today, Brian and I work together but each of us recognizes and values the other's strengths, so we have approached the writing of this book in a slightly unusual way: in the main it is in the first person singular. We felt it was important to present the text in this way for several reasons:

1 because 'I am' are two of the most powerful words a person can say, and they are used frequently throughout the book.

2 because the book follows our practised way of sharing material: Brian shares and teaches through the power of his life story and I share and facilitate through the power of experiential exercise and process. So for you, the reader, it is Brian speaking to you through his stories and me speaking to you through the exercises.

3 because in this form the text flows more naturally and makes for a more enjoyable read.

I hope the book will enable you to find ever-deeper levels of connection to your greatness. For me this is certainly so as I continue to dance with my Life Map!

SANGEETA MAYNE

Time

Stand before me on the sign of infinity.
All you who are of the earth.
With the granting of the law of provocation
comes the application of change.
I will give you this key.
And with this knowledge, please realize,
comes the responsibility of sharing it.
I will show you the way
It is simple.

FROM THE OPENING TO THE MUSICAL *TIME*

INTRODUCTION

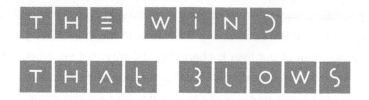

Change in the 21st century

The only future thing of which we can be absolutely certain is that there will be continuing change in our lives.

'Success' comes from learning how to steer the natural changes of life towards the things that we desire.

BRIAN MAYNE

The Winds of Change

We live in a rapidly changing world where the escalating pace of change is greater today than it has been at any other time in recorded history. Every aspect and area of our lives is changing: the way that we work, the way that we mix and interact, the way that we shop and eat. In fact, for the majority of us, all aspects of our day-to-day lives are changing.

Just a few years ago most people's lives were spent in the area in which they were born. They went to school and then served an apprenticeship in that area, which usually led to a job for life in the locality. They were also likely to marry someone from the area and retire and die there.

Now it is the norm to change jobs – and often careers – several times within a twenty- to twenty-five-year work span. People now pack up home and relocate not just nationally but internationally. And it is becoming increasingly common for people to marry several times and have more than one family. It's as if we are now fitting several lifetimes into one.

Never before have so many people needed to cope with so many life-changing decisions in so many different areas on such a consistent and accelerating basis. And herein lies one of the greatest challenges of our times, because *the vast majority of the population fear uncertain change.* We all feel good about the changes that we know or believe are going to make us better off in some way, but the changes that we are uncertain of, or believe may be detrimental, are our greatest fear. Generally, people fear the changes that they feel they cannot steer. The great paradox that so many people experience is that they want things in their life to get better, but at the same time they want to avoid uncertain change.

In reality, the only thing about the future of which we can be absolutely certain is that there will be continuing change in all of our lives. At times the changes may be only minor, while at other times they will be major, but some degree of change is inevitable. We cannot stop it! We cannot even slow it down or delay it. What we can do, however – with a little knowledge, skill and effort – is learn how to direct it.

• • • • • • • • • • • •

The number-one skill in the twenty-first century is learning how to steer the natural changes in life towards the things that we desire.

• • • • • • • • • • • •

Building Windmills

In truth, change is a vital criterion for any form of evolution or growth – for individuals, a community, society as a whole, a country or the entire world. Without 'change' there can be no movement and no growth – either personal or global.

Just as nature is in an ever-continuing cycle of change, so too are human beings. At the very heart of nature there exists a fundamental drive to move onwards and upwards, and this same natural drive is in each one of us. Continuing change is not only a certainty of life but also a necessity for our growth, evolution and general wellbeing. Too much sameness results in stagnation.

• • • • • • • • • • • •

When the winds of change blow, some people build walls, others build windmills.

• • • • • • • • • • • •

Change is like the wind: it is neither good nor bad, friend nor foe; it just is and will continue to be so. It would be naive to expect the wind never to blow again. Instead, we must learn to harness the wind by setting a better sail.

For those who understand how to steer their own ship, set a better sail and flow with the currents, change carries with it the seeds of opportunity. A small minority of people in every age – great leaders, inventors, pioneers, innovators and builders, for example – have discovered this great truth and have learned how to benefit from the winds of change. In fact, every great success in any area of life will have been achieved by learning to steer change.

Because the winds of change are today blowing harder than ever before, they are creating more opportunities for more people to live the life of their choice. We live in a unique time – perhaps even a special time – for never before have so many people enjoyed the freedom to live their lives in the way that they have chosen to. Never before have so many consciously chosen to improve themselves and in so doing raise the quality of life for others around them. Never before have so many people been so aware of their environment and felt such strong motivation to improve it in some way. The evidence of this is apparent in every area of life, from the movement towards a greater health consciousness to the peace campaigns and anti-cruelty protests. On a global basis people are finding their voice, and they are grouping together and insisting on positive change.

Yet there is still much injustice, and there is still war, terrorism and violence in many parts of the world. However, it has always been so and the level of conflict we have at present must be viewed in the broader context of what it has been in the past in order to see the progress we have made.

Never has there been a better, or more important, time for people to learn how to create intentions through steering change and, en masse, create a better world.

. . . .

*Learning how to steer your self in the
direction of your choices brings victory and
self-mastery.*

. . . .

The Coming of Age

Now it is time for the majority of human beings to acquire the ability to steer and maximize change. As an individual you may not have voted to experience a fast-changing world, but the collective drive towards more effective technology has powered a treadmill of change on which many people involuntarily find themselves.

Learning how to steer allows you to benefit from some of the changes and learn from others; it leads your life into calmer waters that flow at a pace of your choosing.

The journey begins by mastering how to steer your *self* – learning how to *lead* your thoughts, feelings, attitudes, actions and habits in the direction of your choices. Victory in these inner areas – or mastery of self – allows you to achieve the creation of your desires, goals and dreams and thus influence your external world.

Life Mapping will show you how to steer the changes affecting your self by learning how to choose which qualities you wish to develop. This is, perhaps, the greatest of all achievements in life. This inner victory – self-mastery or self-leadership – is the ability to choose your response to particular situations, and thus to your life. Self-mastery is the source of all true power and freedom.

Once you master how to steer change from the inside by using your Life Map, the outside automatically follows. The results of your actions are the fruits of your thoughts.

The Unchanging Core

Life Mapping is a unique twenty-first-century personal empowerment system for conscious self-evolution. It is designed to help you to embrace change and grow into a magnificent being who naturally creates a life of heartfelt dreams.

Life Mapping is simple and fun to use, yet is profound in its rewards and expansive in its applications. In the process of creating your own Life Map you create a nucleus of principles and qualities that forms an unchanging core – a central point of inner security that provides stability in a fast-changing environment. This central core becomes your personal 'true north'. It is the compass point by which you steer your course. It enables you to be principle led and purpose driven.

While our situations and circumstances may change greatly – and sometimes lie outside our immediate control – what always remains within our influence, and can therefore be constant, are the principles we choose to live our lives by and the qualities of character that we decide to exhibit.

Life Mapping employs a combination of cutting-edge empowerment technology and ancient wisdom, specifically designed for you to develop your self. It is more than a skill or habit; Life Mapping encompasses a belief system and forms an entire approach to life. The application of its principles and techniques enables you to identify a purpose for your life and to define *who* you choose to become in order to achieve it. In essence, the Life Mapping system directs your focus so that you can create a blueprint for the grandest version of your self – the most magnificent **YOU** that you can imagine.

Life Mapping puts you in the driving seat of your life. It helps you to attain the greatest of all freedoms – the freedom to choose your thoughts, feelings and actions in response to the situations you experience throughout your life.

The very process of creating your Life Map sets you on a path that leads you towards being your best, which naturally enables you to produce your best results in every respect – mentally, emotionally, physically, materially, socially and spiritually. No matter what you are doing, when you feel great you produce great results. Whether working at the office, being at home with the family or out with friends, you will get the most from life when you feel good about your self.

Using your Life Map helps you to develop consciously chosen qualities of character, thereby steering your self to become a person who creates true success in life. The word success can mean different things to different people at different times. To one person success means having a lot of money in the bank, to another it may mean something physical like winning a race or climbing a mountain, while to yet another it can represent living a more purposeful and fulfilling life.

When you examine success more closely, however, it becomes apparent that ultimate success is the ability to live your entire life with true peace of mind, lasting happiness and an experience of abundance – that seems to be what everybody ultimately wants, regardless of the particular path they may take in order to achieve it. This is the real prize that Life Mapping helps you to attain.

• • • • • • • • • • •

We are all in the natural process of becoming; we are all constantly changing. The only thing that stands between us and the life we desire is choosing to become the person who can create it.

• • • • • • • • • • •

The Gift of Your Essence

Creating your Life Map helps you to capture your essence and hold it up as a blueprint for your inner guidance. You crystallize your best thoughts and feelings about your self and this leads you to be proactive in your attitudes and actions, which in turn shape your results. Your Life Map helps you to stay on track and focused on *choosing* who you wish to become, rather than becoming someone by default, like a leaf in the wind, the random result of change.

The Life Mapping system enables you to raise your awareness of The Gift of You. It helps you become clear about what is most important to you – your uniqueness, your purpose – and then to articulate, package and fully realize this gift.

One of Life Mapping's main rewards is achieving balance and harmony in life. It integrates all the aspects of your potential into one focused and balanced whole. Hence, working with the Life Mapping system helps build your self-confidence, self-esteem and self-belief. And with these enhancements come the even greater gains of self-love and self-healing, which over time will produce heightened experiences of peace, fulfilment, happiness and abundance.

Identify what Life Mapping can do for you

Take the opportunity now to identify what you would like to accomplish from creating and using your Life Map. Whilst your answers to the following questions may change as you continue through the process, it is important to have a starting place – a commitment and willingness to head towards a positive focus.

Use a separate journal or notebook for working through all the exercises in the book. In this way you will build up a clear picture of your ongoing journey that you can refer to and add to as you grow into the magnificent YOU.

Ensure you write the answers to the following three questions in a personal and positive way. It is important to trust your own thoughts and feelings here.

1 What are the three main things you would like to accomplish by creating and using your Life Map?

2 Which three things would you most like to change in your life?

3 Which three qualities would you most like to develop?

How Life Mapping Works

Life Mapping works primarily through its ability to connect your consciously chosen desires to your subconscious at a deep level, thereby automatically steering your self towards the achievement of your desires. The subconscious part of your mind acts as your personal autopilot. Each day your subconscious mind processes and actions all the routine functions and requirements in your life, leaving your conscious mind free to ponder many other things. Together your conscious and subconscious minds form a unique and powerful partnership. Your conscious mind is responsible for checking the map, deciding the direction and choosing the destinations in your life, while your subconscious mind is responsible for carrying out the commands and doing whatever is required to get you there.

Life Mapping's effectiveness stems from its ability to communicate your consciously chosen objectives to your subconscious. It helps you to set a target, create a mental map and form a new dominant thought of the person you choose to become. This communication to your sub-conscious is achieved through activating both the left and right sides of your brain (the logical and the emotional, respectively), thereby forming a deep whole-brain connection to your subconscious.

Life Balance

Generally, the right side of our brain is visionary, expansive, creative, emotional and intuitive. It is the side we use for imagining where, what and who we choose to be. It is often referred to as our leadership brain. The left side of our brain is our management brain. It possesses the qualities of symmetry and order. With it we bring structure, past experience and harmony to our lives, and typically we use this side to identify our most effective course of action or path.

The process of creating your Life Map activates your right brain and enables you to visualize what you desire to achieve, while your left brain is employed to define and state intentions in a succinct form that will have maximum impact on your subconscious.

The end result is a balanced 'mandala' – a defined set of statements or affirmations for your left brain, with corresponding picture symbols or visualizations for your right brain.

When both halves of our brain, and the qualities they produce, are balanced, we become extremely effective at steering the changes to create our physical desires, choosing who we want to become, and achieving true happiness.

We are designed to function best when there is a balance between the two halves of our brain, a condition which is present in all true geniuses. From birth up until about age five most of us have a good balance between both halves. Consequently, it is at this time that we learn the fastest. However, from around five onwards we are gradually conditioned by the influences of the world around us and become more and more left-brain dominant. In the process we often lose a degree of our effectiveness.

Using your Life Map on a regular basis will enable you to rebalance the two halves of your brain and regain the ability you had as a child to learn much faster.

Getting the Best From This Book

The technique of Life Mapping is designed to be a complete system for your self-development. The essential points are presented in the form of bold statements within the text.

I recommend that you read the entire book first and complete all the exercises, and then review and update your Life Map at three-month intervals. Evolving your Life Map is important, because as you develop your chosen qualities there will always be a 'what's next?' in your development if you are to continue to evolve consciously as a person. When updating, either you can revisit the key points and exercises in each chapter before going to the Life Mapping technique text, or, if you feel confident in your understanding, you can go directly to the Appendix at the back of the book where you will find a summary of the process.

Preparing For Your Inner Journey

Before you embark on your journey and the creation of your Life Map, I have a simple but important suggestion to help you achieve the best results: create a Possibility Consciousness.

Our conscious mind is always questioning, evaluating and filtering information by way of our current viewpoints and beliefs. While this is a great benefit in life generally, in specific situations it can be a huge drawback, because if you decide that certain information is of no relevance, you literally start to filter out entire sections of it and may miss something of great importance. I therefore suggest that you create a space in your mind called 'possibility', and into this space place all the information, ideas, principles and concepts you are about to read. Then once you get to the end of the book, you will be in an informed position to evaluate how Life Mapping can best serve you and bring you the success you seek.

PART I

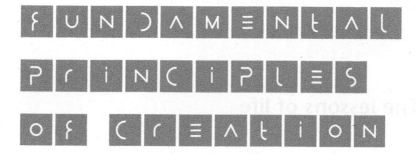

FUNDAMENTAL
PRINCIPLES
OF CREATION

CHAPTER 1

The lessons of life

The real voyage of discovery consists not in seeking new landscapes, but in having new eyes.

MARCEL PROUST

Paradigms – Our Pictures of Life

Take a look at the picture below. What do you see?

Some of you will see a word quite quickly. Others will take a little longer. And for those of you who still cannot see one, turn the book upside down and frame the top and bottom edges of the diagram with your hands. You will then see clearly that what might have appeared at first glance as just a jumble of random shapes and meaningless patterns is actually a word – FLY.

Most people find that it is the dark colours that stand out when they first look at the picture. Only when they include the white space around the patterns do they become aware of the word FLY and realize a higher level of meaning or order in the picture.

This process, the experience of mentally moving from the chaos of random shapes to a realization of order or meaning – of moving from one level of understanding to another – is known as a *paradigm shift*.

• • • • • • • • • • • •

A paradigm shift is a complete and sudden switch of perception from seeing something one way to suddenly seeing it quite differently.

• • • • • • • • • • • •

Whether you were aware of the word FLY quickly or it took you a little longer, the actual dawning of the realization would have happened in just a fraction of a moment. And it is in this moment of realization that the paradigm shift occurs.

We will each experience paradigm shifts at various times throughout our life. The word 'paradigm' comes from the Greek *paradeigma*, meaning pattern. It represents a pattern or picture of understanding that we have, a mental structure of ideas or beliefs that we hold. When we experience a paradigm shift it means we suddenly change our opinion and viewpoint.

Blueprints For Understanding

We form paradigms about everything – the people we meet, the places we go to and the experiences we have. We form paradigms about the world in general, and about ourselves specifically. They represent more than just our opinions – they are our blueprints for understanding and as such allow us to navigate our daily life with minimal conscious effort.

Generally speaking, when you wake up in the morning you don't need to think about who you are and how you deal with the world; by and large you just get on with your day. This is possible because you have a series of paradigms – picture blueprints – in your head that tell you who you are and how you fit in. They are the pictures that you have built up over years of experiences in different areas of your life and they represent your current level of understanding and awareness. Your paradigms therefore form a blueprint for your subconscious which it uses to shape your automatic actions or responses to the situations you encounter.

• • • • • • • • • • •

We form paradigms about everything. They are our blueprints for understanding and our route maps to success.

• • • • • • • • • • •

Personal Paradigm Shifts

The experience of undergoing a paradigm shift is the equivalent of updating one or more of these blueprints to a higher level of accuracy and realization. The personal paradigm shifts that are most notable to us are usually those that are triggered by intense emotional experiences. Sometimes these feel positive, sometimes negative. Changing schools or moving home often triggers a paradigm shift. Positive experiences such as getting married or having a baby can most definitely result in one. It is usual for people to see themselves and their lives completely differently after such events.

Likewise, many painful or negative experiences – redundancy, the break-up of a relationship or the loss of someone close – can also trigger a paradigm shift.

If you've been in a serious accident or an emergency situation – one that causes you to think deeply about your life, when your life flashes before your eyes – you may at that time have experienced a paradigm shift. Such moments allow us to see ourselves and our lives more clearly, to realize what is most important to us, to learn valuable lessons about life.

Several of my friends who have suddenly found themselves in intense situations have, through the experience, had a realization of what they value most in their life, such as their family, friendships or some form of faith. Often they are very different people after the experience. The paradigm shift causes them not only to see things differently, but also to feel, behave and act differently.

Distorted Paradigms

Some years ago, while out for a drink I bumped into two old friends that I hadn't seen for some time. Whilst chatting, I glanced round the bar and noticed this odd-looking man standing off to one side. My first thought was that he seemed out of place. It was a really young, fun bar, and this guy was much, much older than the other customers.

At first I thought he was staring at the floor in front of me, but then I realized he was staring at the legs of the two girls I was talking to. They were both good looking and as it was a Saturday night they had dressed up for it and looked great. This man couldn't keep his eyes off them. As I watched him he looked up past their legs and caught my eye. In that brief moment of direct contact he became uncomfortable, picked up his drink and walked off. I turned back to continue my conversation with the girls, but no more than a moment had passed when I noticed out of the corner of my eye that the man had come back. He was standing in the same place and staring at my friends again.

I then did something that I have since learned to be fatal. I took the moral high ground and *judged* that this person was wrong. I decided that I would do to him what he was doing to others, so I turned and faced him head on and stared back at him.

My expression would clearly have told him of my unhappiness, for I held the most intense stare. Within a few moments it began to work. He became uncomfortable and started glancing at the floor, and I could see that he was starting to sweat slightly as he fidgeted nervously from one foot to the other while wringing his hands.

I was giving this man only two choices: come over and say something to me or stop staring and go away. My goal was clear: I wanted him to leave. So I just held my ground and firmly fixed my focus. Just as I was getting to the point of melting this man with my laser-beam eyes, one of the girls I was talking to went over to him, kissed him on the cheek and said, 'Thanks for bringing us over, John. I'm sorry you're not feeling too well. We'll be ready to go in about half an hour.'

Suddenly, I had a huge paradigm shift. I gained a greater clarity of the reality. The picture or paradigm that I had been seeing the situation through was very different from the reality of the situation. My paradigm was of a dirty old man who liked to stare at young girls. In reality he was a friend of the family who had driven the girls miles across town to the bar and was about to give them a lift home. Because he wasn't feeling very well he had stood quietly in the corner, but he had still managed to keep a protective eye on his two young friends.

• • • • • • • • • • • •

We make judgements through our paradigms.

• • • • • • • • • • • •

When I look back on the experience now I still feel a slight twinge of embarrassment, but the story highlights some important insights about paradigm shifts.

What changed for me in that instant I realized the reality of the situation? Most people spot straightaway that how I was *seeing* the situation instantly changed – but what about my *attitude* and *behaviour?* How do you think they were influenced?

With the shift in my paradigm came a complete change in my body posture and attitude. I became open and humble and my behaviour moved from offensive to passive as I tried to apologize to this man, buy him a drink and get us a table where we could all sit down together.

• • • • • • • • • • • •

*When your paradigm changes, so too does
your attitude and behaviour.*

• • • • • • • • • • • •

Changing Your Paradigm

Through the course of our work Sangeeta and I regularly meet people in our workshops who are to some degree or other struggling to change something about themselves. Typically, they want to change their habits and behaviours or their attitudes and feelings towards something or someone.

The first step in the Life Mapping workshops, as here in the book, is to help people understand that in order to achieve a desired change in attitude and behaviour they must first create a paradigm aligned to the desired change.

Your paradigm is the blueprint that your subconscious reads so that it can select your behaviour. Any time you are not consciously making an effort to choose, your subconscious automatically acts in accordance with your dominant paradigm. The collection of all of your paradigm pictures is like an autopilot which your subconscious reverts to when guiding you through life.

Every once in a while – on occasions such as New Year's Eve – many people decide to make changes. The approach that most of them follow is to grab hold of the 'controls of their behaviour' and, through sheer willpower, stop drinking, swearing, smoking or whatever habit they wish to give up and steer themselves in a new direction. However, unless they also change the paradigm they hold of their self – the blueprint for their habits – their success is often short lived. Usually one of two things happens. For some the habit is too strong and they soon give in. Others overcome the habit initially and hold to their intention. Then, after a while, when they are feeling pretty good about themselves, they relax their grip on the controls of their behaviour. And because the paradigm of themselves is still one of a person who is drinking, swearing or smoking, their autopilot steers them straight back to the old habit.

• • • • • • • • • • • • • • •

*There can be no lasting change in your self unless
there is also a shift in your paradigm.*

• • • • • • • • • • • • • • •

Raising Your Self-Awareness

Without question, the greatest paradigm shifts I have experienced have
been those which focused on some aspect of my self. Sometimes they
were a little dramatic and painful and sometimes hugely exciting. Always
they were ultimately beneficial because they helped me to see more
clearly. The things about ourselves that are most painful for us to look at
are those that are the hardest for us to see. Often we have a cloudy,
distorted, or even totally false picture of our self or of other people and
the world around us.

• • • • • • • • • • • • • • •

We see life not so much as it is but rather as we are.

• • • • • • • • • • • • • • •

We each have a unique paradigm through which we see life. Sometimes
this can cause us to distort or delete information from our senses. This
is why three different people can witness the same accident and yet give
three very different statements to the police. It is why we don't all laugh
at the same jokes and like the same fashions.

A *personal paradigm shift* about your self means seeing your self more
clearly: seeing your ways of being – your behaviours, motivations or true
feelings – and the results that they create in your life and how they
impact on the lives of those around you. It is the process of raising your
self-awareness.

Life Mapping helps you create a clear picture of your self and your purpose – a snapshot of you being your best, a paradigm of personal success for your subconscious to steer towards. Living your Life Map enables you to make your new desired paradigm the dominant one which your subconscious will revert to when on autopilot.

My greatest paradigm shift came at about age twenty-nine when all of the important areas of my life – such as home, business and social life – seemed to collapse at the same time. I found the shock overwhelming. For most of my life, certainly since my teens, I had been playing a game. It's called 'Let's Pretend', and the rules are that you have to pretend that you're not pretending. Millions of people play this game, each of them pretending to be someone they are not. I used to pretend that I was confident when really I was desperately insecure. I pretended I was outgoing when deep down I was shy. I pretended to be happy when actually I felt sad. I wore a mask of bravado, a veil of false confidence to hide and compensate for my feelings of insecurity.

I wore the mask for so long that I even forgot I was wearing it – not because it fitted so well but because I had become desensitized to its presence. When my life crashed, the intensity of the experience had the effect of tearing the mask away. I then saw my self for who I really was. It shook me to acknowledge that I was not who I was pretending to be.

I had never really wanted to look at the truth, to acknowledge that my confidence had always come from what I owned or controlled. When all of that was lost, so was my confidence and I plummeted to an all-time low. Seeing my self as I really was and accepting that I was insecure was one of the hardest things I have ever done. But it was also one of the most rewarding, for once I saw clearly, I was greatly empowered to make changes and improvements.

• • • • • • • • • • • • •

Even the world's greatest marksman cannot
hit the target if he doesn't know what it is.

• • • • • • • • • • • •

After I recovered from the pain and tears of my realization I took a long, clear look at my life and my self. It was then that I had the first of many positive paradigm shifts about my situation. I saw that while I had worn a mask of false confidence for most of my life, there were, every so often, specific times when I had not. There were times when I had not tried to impress anyone, times when I had felt no need to put on a false front or pretence.

As I looked more closely I started to see specific times when I had just been me, times when I had just been my self, my True Self. The realization dawned that it was on these occasions that I had had the most fun, experienced the most joy, achieved my best results, got on best with other people and felt the best about my self. Sometimes these experiences would last for only a short period but, regardless of the time-frame, the results they produced were always great.

Magical Moments

There are many different names that people have for these moments. Athletes refer to 'being in the Zone' or 'being in the Field'; some people refer to 'being in the Flow'. They are the moments when everything clicks into place, when things come together with ease, naturally, like they are meant to be. Most people have experienced one of those moments when they feel they are in the right place at the right time, knowing just the right thing to say or do. Sometimes the experience may last for only a moment, but in that moment everything flows like magic. In fact, we often call them *magical moments*. They are the moments when we feel our most *natural* and magical.

Identify positive and negative feelings

Think back now about a magical moment that you have had.

Choose the first one that comes to you, and allow your self to relive it in your mind. Reconnect to your memory and how you felt at that time.

Once you are in touch with the experience, make a list in your journal of the feelings, thoughts and personal qualities that were present for you in that moment.

I have run this exercise with thousands of people and the answers that they give are always remarkably similar. The words frequently cited are: peaceful, confident, positive, open minded, in control of self, energized, happy, calm, motivated, natural – together with self-belief, love, joy, freedom, abundance and clarity.

Now think back to a time when things weren't going so well, one of those 'off days' when things aren't flowing and relationships aren't working. Then list what your main thoughts, feelings and qualities were on those days.

Again, I have found that these answers are also extremely alike. Words that often come up include: confused, stressed, insecure, negative, closed, trapped, powerless, drained, sad, tense, lethargic, doubtful, frustrated, angry, fearful.

The reality for most of us is that our lives are a mixture of both lists. Some days we get more of the positive thoughts, feelings and qualities; other days we have more of the negative. Life is a mixture of pain and pleasure. Some people experience more of one, some more of the other.

• • • • • • • • • • • • • • • •

*For many of us a negative type of moment may feel
more normal, but that does not mean it is natural.*

• • • • • • • • • • • • • • • •

My paradigm shift allowed me not only to see past my mask to my actual way of being, but also to realize that although the magical moments I had experienced were very different, the qualities in each were essentially the same.

My most important realization was understanding *that nothing happens by accident.* The magical moments we experience may appear to be random and chance, but as we raise our awareness and see through to deeper levels of reality we discover that such moments are a direct result of our specific ways of being.

• • • • • • • • • • • • • • • •

*Our way of being is made up of our thoughts, feelings,
attitudes, actions and habits. It is our way of being
that creates and attracts our magical moments.*

• • • • • • • • • • • • • •

Once I had this realization my goal became clear: to increase the number of magical moments in my life by cultivating the 'ways of being' that produce them. It was through striving to achieve this goal that I gained the knowledge of the fundamental principles that empower Life Mapping. And this is what I want to pass on to you – that you have the power to choose to experience any of the magical moment qualities you wrote on your list at any time, anywhere, and in response to any circumstance. Because you are always free to develop any aspect of your self, Life Mapping provides the perfect framework in which to exercise fully this freedom.

Questions to raise your self-awareness

Look again at the two lists you have written. They will give you an insight into your paradigm of your self and the way in which you view the world around you.

To create your Life Map you will need to know which aspects of your self you wish to develop. Here are some questions for you to reflect on.

1. When you look at your self, what do you see? Using your journal, describe the picture you see of your self. Take into account what you say to your self on a regular basis and how you genuinely feel about your self, because all of this makes up your picture paradigm.

2. What is your paradigm about life? Again, include your major viewpoints, how you feel and common phrases you use. For example, someone who goes through life thinking 'life's a breeze' approaches life very differently from someone who thinks 'life's a bitch'. Be careful not to fall into the trap of describing what you would like to be true rather than what is – that would be playing the 'pretend game'. One way to ensure you've seen past your mask and captured the truth is to observe your self over several days, noting your behaviour and attitudes in the various situations you face.

3. What are the different masks that you wear for your different roles in life?

4. Are your attitudes and behaviours in alignment with what you believe to be your paradigms? If they are, great; you know you've got to the truth. If they are not, ask your self which paradigms align best with your attitudes and behaviours. Look again at your self and your life with a real openness and willingness and a desire to see the truth. Remember, raising awareness of your truth can sometimes be

painful. Go through this process only if you are willing to move forward. It is also important to respect and honour your truth without any self-judgement. This exercise becomes counter productive if it results in destructive self-criticism.

True Success

Each of the positive ways of being that you listed is a choice. Each entry is an aspect of a magical moment and each can be consciously chosen.

• • • • • • • • • • • •

The path to true success is through developing the ability to make conscious choices about your thoughts, feelings and behaviours, regardless of your situation or circumstances.

• • • • • • • • • • •

There are probably as many different definitions of success as there are people who have thought about it. Everyone has their own unique paradigm of what success means. My own definition of success is to go through life with peace of mind, happiness and abundance. I believe this to be true success.

Abundance begins with a paradigm that believes *I have enough*. 'Enough' is different for everyone. What is enough for me might not be enough for you, and vice versa, but as long as you experience having enough you are not in want and will therefore feel abundant.

So abundance begins as a state of *being*, an attitude, and as such relates to anything in life. Abundance is not really about how much of something you have, such as wealth or love, but about your ability to give and receive it freely – allowing it to flow into and out of your life. It is the feeling of being full and satisfied, of not *needing* to chase after this thing. In this way you are free to receive it and to give it without attachment.

Love is a classic example. Do you know anyone who holds love in scarcity, like it should be rationed or even reserved for that someone special who has yet to come along? Think about it; we say *love makes the world go round*, but in reality we hold back on giving it fully and freely and instead act as if it were in short supply.

Abundance is one aspect of success, but it is achieved only in combination with others. Without the inner successes of learning how to create happiness and peace of mind, all external forms of success have little meaning or satisfaction in the long term. Some people become incredibly successful in one area of their life – their work, perhaps – but are unsuccessful at making themselves truly happy.

Over many years Sangeeta and I have regularly asked in our seminars why it is that some people achieve greater peace of mind and more happiness and abundance than others. The response we often get is that such people have just been lucky in some way, that success comes from being born into the right family, getting the right education, meeting the right people or having the right breaks.

I'll agree that any of those factors can give someone an obvious advantage, but the fact of the matter is that history is filled with the names of those who had the worst possible start and yet, against the odds, went on to success beyond most people's wildest dreams. Henry Ford, for instance, came from a poor family and didn't learn to read and write until late in life. And Thomas Edison, probably the greatest inventor of the twentieth century, had only three months of formal education and no scientific training.

One of the greatest examples of overcoming disadvantages to succeed is Abraham Lincoln, who was born into abject poverty, had just a few months' schooling, and in his first job split wooden rails for a living. And in more recent times, both Nelson Mandela and Mother Teresa started with next to nothing but through genuine desire born out of a deep sense of purpose, developed their self and achieved wonders.

In contrast, pick up the newspaper, turn on the TV or listen to the radio and you are likely to learn about the downfall of someone who started off with all the material advantages yet failed to learn certain lessons about life and ultimately lost everything.

One of the most important lessons we can learn from this is:

• • • • • • • • • • • • • • •

Success is not an accident. Success is on purpose.

• • • • • • • • • • • • • • •

Success happens for a reason. It has a formula that we can learn and recreate. Lasting success in any area of life is the natural result of a three-stage process: thinking successful thoughts, creating successful feelings and taking successful actions.

Building a successful life begins by holding a successful paradigm. Living your Life Map and holding a successful paradigm enables you to become a person who can create a successful life. In order to create your Life Map it is important first to have a clear picture of your overall paradigm of life so that you can ensure it empowers rather than limits you.

The Lessons of Life

Take a good look around you and you will see a vast range of levels of success in the various areas of people's lives. At one end are those who spend almost their entire life predominantly experiencing the negative list of feelings and qualities mentioned earlier, and at the other end are those who have learned how to live mostly with the feelings and qualities from the positive, magical moments list. In reality, most of us probably live in between these two extremes of our true and false self, experiencing a myriad of different levels and types of success.

• • • • • • • • • • • • • • • • • • •

*What separates people into different levels of success
are not the circumstances of their birth or early years
but the lessons of life that they have learned.*

• • • • • • • • • • • • • • • • • • •

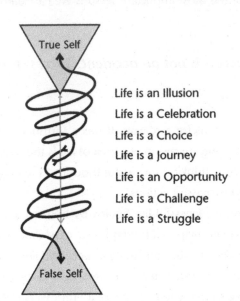

Life is an Illusion

Life is a Celebration

Life is a Choice

Life is a Journey

Life is an Opportunity

Life is a Challenge

Life is a Struggle

Life is like a huge school in which you don't move up to the next level
until you have learned the lessons of the one you are on. Each lesson is
taught through life experiences. The situations we encounter, the
emotions we feel and the results of our behaviour gradually teach us
what works and what doesn't. Formal learning involves gaining
knowledge and skills, but without the challenge of life experience we
never gain real wisdom.

Each lesson helps us form a more accurate paradigm of reality and
thus gives us greater influence over the direction of our desires. Each
level has its own paradigm and each lesson is like a piece of a jigsaw; it

is only when we have several pieces, or lessons, that we are able to see the bigger picture of success. Sometimes we may have an almost complete paradigm of success, but if one or two vital pieces are missing we cannot move on.

There can be no cheating. All of those who try to cut corners will find that their successes are incomplete or short lived. This can be seen in people who suddenly come into wealth that is beyond the lessons they have learned – they often slip back to their previous level. As the saying goes, 'A fool and his money are soon parted.'

Discover your true paradigm

When I first started my journey of personal development I explored my overall paradigm of life and was a little shocked to realize that it wasn't quite what I wanted it to be, which was: You make your own success in life. In reality, my behaviour and my attitudes and reactions to life were more in alignment with the paradigm Life is a struggle. I soon saw even deeper to another paradigm I had: Money equals happiness. I looked back for further evidence to try and understand where these paradigms might have come from.

I saw that when I was growing up I was strongly influenced by beliefs that one had to work hard for success, that success was measured in money, and that this was what ultimately brought happiness in life. My mother, a single parent, worked hard, struggled to make ends meet and devoted every spare penny she had to ensuring her children received the best opportunities to 'succeed' in life. She would say time and again, 'Life's a struggle; you have to work very hard to get anywhere in life.' I saw clearly how this paradigm had shaped my beliefs. It had constantly caused me to create results which required me to work hard and experience struggle.

Growing up with the paradigm that money equals happiness drove me to strive for a materially successful career. In fact, enjoyment of my career was secondary to the status and success they represented. My justification was that I couldn't be happy without the material success.

The defining moment, my paradigm shift, came with the break-up of my marriage. It was an intense emotional experience. I felt as if my whole world had fallen apart. I realized I was not happy – I was materially successful but miserable. How could this be? My paradigm of true success changed in a heartbeat and it was at that moment that my search to redefine what success and happiness meant began.

Define your overall paradigm of life

To define your personal paradigm, go back to the questions for raising self-awareness on page 26. If you haven't already answered them, take some time to do so now.

Then take another look in your journal at your lists of positive (magical moment) and negative qualities (see page 24). Now try to extract the essence of what you have written and capture it in a statement which best defines your overall paradigm of life. Then record it in your journal. Some people find it helps to take a short journey into their past in order to test the validity of their paradigm. Now ask your self if your desired paradigm is in alignment with what really matters to you and with what you want to achieve in life. If your answer is 'yes', that's great; it means that your current paradigm empowers you to move forward in your life. If your answer is 'no', then construct a new paradigm that is in alignment and note it in your journal.

The following chapter will show you how to alter your paradigm by fine-tuning your beliefs

Tuning in to your potential

*We were born to make manifest the glory of God
that is within us.*

It is not just in some of us; it is in everyone.

*As we let our light shine, we unconsciously give other
people permission to do the same.*

*As we are liberated from our own fear,
our presence automatically liberates others.*

**WRITTEN BY MARIANNE WILLIAMSON
FOR NELSON MANDELA'S 1994 INAUGURAL SPEECH**

Pure Potential

How would you respond if I were to say that 'understanding and applying the information in this book could be one of the most important things in your life'? When I have made this statement in the past it has triggered numerous responses, ranging from belief that it could make a huge difference through to strong disagreement.

However, the simple fact is that over the years Sangeeta and I have both witnessed thousands of people who have had life-changing experiences as a result of this material. They have experienced a paradigm shift about themselves and their lives that then led them to take action to evolve their self and their life to a higher level.

Our greatest gift is our free will – we are free to choose our own path, free to improve and evolve our self.

Thoreau said it well: *'I know of no more encouraging fact than the unquestionable ability of man to elevate his life by a conscious effort.'*

Most doctors, scientists and experts on human potential agree that at birth we each have the ability to excel, to live a life of true happiness with peace of mind and abundance.

One of the keys to attaining this state is to 'realize' or know this potential. Those who do, operate from the paradigm 'I have the power to achieve whatever I truly believe.'

Some time ago I came across an ancient story of two Indian sages who sit watching a crowded bazaar. One turns to the other and, pointing to the crowd with his outstretched arm, says, 'See, all here have got rupees in their bundles – but how to open the knot, *that* they do not know, and therefore they are paupers.'

The great realization and paradigm shift for me was that *I was already successful*. All I needed to do was figure out the combination that would unlock my potential and unleash my ability.

Your Mental Map of Meaning

The human brain is more powerful than even the most sophisticated computer. We possess mental abilities that science has only just begun to explore and other abilities that are still a complete mystery. However, even though we have almighty power within our minds and the ability to achieve greatness within our lives, when we are born we come into the world as pure and unshaped potential.

Even the most powerful computer is only as effective as the information put into it. As is said in the computer industry, 'Garbage in equals garbage out.' When you receive a new computer you can turn it on and run it, but until you load a program it's not really able to do very much.

We have an urge to reproduce, an instinct to cry if we are in discomfort, a fear of loud noises, and numerous influences of character, none of which is set or fixed but is instead like the raw material from which we construct our master operating program. Everything else has to be conditioned, learned and developed.

Sadly, like the computer that is fed poor material, people who are born into a harsh environment often assimilate negative aspects and begin to form their own limitations. We begin programming our super-computer brain from the moment we are born. We achieve this amazing feat through the experiences that we have and the meaning that we automatically attach to each one.

Right now, each of you reading this has a 'mental map of meaning' constructed from the paradigm pictures you have generated over the years. Your map informs you *who you are* and *how you deal with the world* around you. It allows you to carry out repetitive tasks with minimal conscious effort.

But at birth your map of meaning is comparatively blank. It is believed that at this very young age our senses are just a jumble of fuzzy energy patterns. Gradually we learn to define these patterns and begin to focus our sight, sharpen our hearing and develop a sense of touch, taste and smell. With the energy of innate curiosity driving us forward, we start to explore our surroundings, with each experience adding detail to our internal picture of our external world.

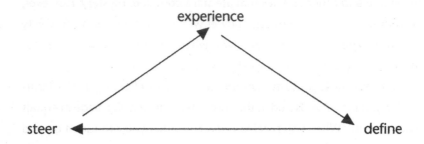

The work of creating our mental map is an ongoing process. From the moment we have an experience we begin to question. The questions that we would normally ask ourselves at this primary stage of our development are most likely to be along the lines of: 'What just happened?' or 'What does that mean to me?' At the most basic level the question we are going to ask is, 'Did that experience give me pleasure or did it give me pain?' The moment that we answer that question we label the experience, calling it either pain or pleasure, and fill in a little more detail on our mental map of meaning about what we like and don't like.

In the final step in the process our subconscious automatically steers us towards the things we have labelled 'pleasure' and away from the things we have labelled 'pain'.

Although our fantastic personal autopilot allows us to flow through life without continuous conscious effort, there is a danger that while we are young and still learning and growing we will place the wrong label on an experience. If we mistakenly call something pain we may then avoid it for the rest of our life when in fact it could have been the very best thing for us.

• • • • • • • • • • •

*So many people fall short of their true
potential because their fear holds them back
in some way.*

• • • • • • • • • • •

A wise man once said, 'That which we persist in becomes easier – not because the nature of the thing changes, but because our ability to do it increases.'

Something I have done a great deal of over the years is public speaking; it has never really scared me. And I often found this puzzling, because deep down I was actually quite timid. I can remember my father telling someone once that I was 'a little chicken hearted'.

When I looked back to trace the source of my confidence in public speaking I saw that it had started at about age ten when my father got me to take the microphone and call out the numbers for the bingo in our amusement arcade. I don't suppose my father could have ever imagined he was helping to prepare me for a future in public speaking; it was simply something that I could do to help him. The upside for me was that the old ladies who were our best customers thought that this was cute and they made a fuss of me.

Hence, from an early age I started to attach pleasure to the experience of public speaking. I have therefore steered my self – sometimes consciously, sometimes unconsciously – to do more and more of it. And although I wasn't always that polished when I first started speaking in public, it did give me a good feeling and I felt motivated to do more of it. The more often I presented, the easier it became, the more I improved and the greater pleasure I attached to it.

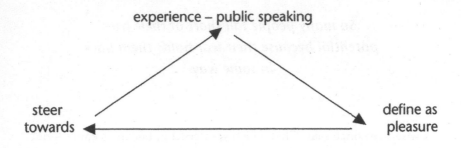

experience – public speaking

steer
towards

define as
pleasure

In contrast to my experience, public speaking for most people represents their greatest pain. In surveys of what people fear most, it always comes near the top. Most people don't even remember where this fear came from in the first place. Usually it begins way back when they were very young.

Imagine this situation. A teacher asks a straightforward question such as 'Where is Italy?' All the kids put their hands up and the teacher chooses one at the back, who answers, 'It's on page 26 in the atlas, miss.' Now, the answer's correct as far as the child is concerned – Italy is indeed on page 26 in the atlas – but it's not the answer the teacher wanted. She thinks the child is playing about and says something like, 'Don't be so stupid.' Although the teacher doesn't mean any harm, nevertheless everyone in the class laughs. And now the child is thinking, 'I just felt stupid; I just felt embarrassed; I just felt not good enough. I will never ever again volunteer for public speaking because all it brings me is pain.'

From that point on the child's subconscious autopilot begins to steer away from anything that looks like, smells like or could even be disguised as an opportunity to speak out in public.

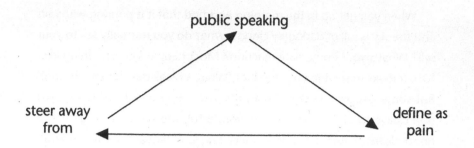

public speaking

steer away from

define as pain

A Check-Up From the Neck Up

Part 1

We all form a mental map of meaning from the collective of our paradigms, and our subconscious mind constantly reads this map to navigate us through life. But there are a million different labels that we can place on a million different experiences, so the challenge is to get it right. Both maturity and success help us to put the right labels on each experience.

• • • • • • • • • • •

The greater the accuracy of our map of meaning, the greater our ability to navigate life and benefit ourselves.

• • • • • • • • • • •

Please understand that the map of paradigms that you have in your head is not a literal representation of the world around you but a representation of your personal and unique world. It represents *your truth* but not necessarily the reality that is *the truth.* Learning how to separate fact from fiction, what really happened rather than our version of what happened, is how we create accurate maps. In other words, the way that you see something is just that; it may or may not be the actual reality.

When you get up in the morning and find that it is pouring with rain and the sky is full of dark-grey clouds, what do you normally say to your self? What's your immediate reaction? Most people say something like: 'Oh, it looks miserable out there!' or 'What a bleak day; it's depressing!' But some people will say, 'Great, it's just the excuse I wanted; now I don't have to ...', or even, 'How wonderful, Mother Earth is getting a good cleanse.' And if you live where rain is essential for your survival, you will positively bless its arrival.

The key is to set aside the *fact* (it is raining) and understand that the rest is just your interpretation, your fiction, your opinion, your truth. Each of us will give the fact that it is raining a meaning, and in just the same way we give meaning to everything else in life.

* * * * * * * * * * * *

You give everything in life a meaning, so you might as well choose meanings that serve you well.

* * * * * * * * * * * *

Play the 'Choose My Truth' game

In this game you practise the art of consciously choosing your truth for one whole day. Here's how.

Start the day with some mental relaxation and preparation. Close your eyes and take three long, deep, slow breaths. Breathe in through your nose and repeat to your self the word RELAX as you exhale through your mouth.

Keeping your eyes closed, say the words 'I give everything in my life its meaning.' Repeat this phrase seven times in all, each time giving the words more meaning and feeling.

Now run through your day ahead at fast speed for a few minutes. Imagine it going just the way you want it to. See your self approaching every situation with clarity and objectivity – confident and in control of your ability to respond to all situations, mentally, physically and emotionally. See the day being thoroughly enjoyable and successful for all concerned.

When you have finished say the words, 'May what happens be for the greater good of all.' Then gently take another three deep breaths as you start to become aware of your self and your surroundings again. Open your eyes on the third deep breath and stretch your arms up to the ceiling and push your feet firmly into the ground to ensure you are fully back in the present moment.

Make 'I give everything in my life its meaning' your dominant thought as you go through your day. Repeat it to your self – and out loud – as often as possible. Make it your mantra with every experience, person, event and situation you encounter. Practise the art of separating fact from fiction. Check that the meaning you have given to an experience is what actually happened or what was actually said. So often we place our paradigm over the top of a situation and then, through it, create all sorts of meanings that can often be inaccurate or false.

If you feel the meaning you have doesn't serve your greatest good – creating peace of mind, happiness and abundance – choose one that does.

Take time out towards the end of the day to capture your experiences in your journal. Note what might have changed for you during the day, what worked when you played this game and what didn't, and what was missing for you.

With practice you'll find you can quickly and automatically choose the best meaning in most situations. This will help build your map of meaning and bring a higher level of clarity and responsibility to your thinking, attitudes, behaviours and results.

The Human Radio

Have you ever listened to a radio that is slightly out of tune, that is picking up the main station but the sound is a little distorted? Imagine, if you had spent your whole life listening to just one radio that happened to be slightly out of tune, would you actually know it was out of tune? Probably not, if you had nothing to compare it with. I believe this is a good analogy for how a vast number of people go through life; they are *like a human radio*, filled with potential but slightly out of tune. The main station called 'life' is playing, but the interference of negativity distorts their reception.

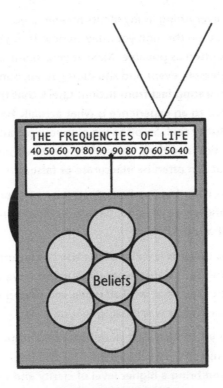

THE HUMAN RADIO

For me, one of the saddest thoughts is the realization that 'The vast majority of the population will go to their grave with their best music still unsung.' Most people never even begin to realize their true potential.

If you have a radio that is slightly out of tune, how much of an adjustment do you need to make on the dial to correct it – a little or a lot? Only a little. Likewise, the smallest adjustments to your self can make the biggest difference to your life. All you need do is tune into what you really want instead of listening to the interference.

Often we act as if our radio were stuck on just one station. We say that it plays a sad song and that it's not our fault. We say that it's due to pre-programming, our past, our upbringing or to the circumstances we find ourselves in. But in truth, our radio is never stuck. It is always ready to play whatever song we wish – all it requires is our desire, willingness and determination to tune it.

Many people are afraid to fiddle with the dials. They fear the change that would come from tuning in to an unfamiliar frequency. Others stick their head in the sand of denial and announce to the world, and themselves, that their radio isn't capable of playing successful music. Sometimes they even engage in destructive self-sabotaging behaviour.

Just imagine that you have the most powerful, fantastic, wonderful radio ever conceived, but that you don't like the music it is playing. What do you do?

Do you become fatalistic and say, 'That's it, I'm destined to experience this rubbish for the rest of my life'? Do you smash and destroy it? Do you deny that there is anything wrong with it and try to fool your self into believing that it's playing the best music that it can? Or do you simply and gently, without any real effort or stress, tune in to another frequency, one that's playing the kind of music you like? Through the process of creating your Life Map you will automatically tune into the station playing your greatest music.

Raise awareness of your current reality

Take some time out here to raise your awareness of your current reality by making a note in your journal of the ways in which you stop your self from fine-tuning your radio. Perhaps you use some of the following excuses:

- I'm too busy/there's never enough time
- I can't help it/it's not my fault
- I/It's not important enough
- I'm not strong/good enough

Note, too, the ways in which you avoid taking action – for example by:

- denying there is anything wrong
- hiding behind what you know you can do
- keeping your self busy doing stuff
- procrastinating and put things off

Now make a note of your fears and concerns – for example:

- self-doubt
- low self-esteem
- fear of failure
- fear of the unknown

Tuning In Through Beliefs

The frequencies or stations of life are represented on a radio by the wavebands. On each waveband there is a needle. We could call this needle our success indicator. It points out which of the frequencies of life we are picking up on, for we are always successfully picking up on something, even if it's not what we consciously wanted. In order to tune into another, or better, frequency, all we need to do is move our success indicator by turning the dial. And the central dial of our human radio is our beliefs.

· · · · · · · · · · · · ·

By making fine adjustments to our beliefs we bring our paradigm of life into focus.

· · · · · · · · · · · · ·

Our beliefs are like the valve that turns our potential on or off. Whatever you believe to be true for you *will* be true for you in your experience. Many of our beliefs are formed through the meaning that we attach to the experiences that we have. Once we decide what something means and no longer question that decision, it becomes a belief.

A belief is a feeling of certainty that we have about something. Strong beliefs are convictions and weak beliefs are opinions but, regardless of its strength, a belief is always a predetermined idea that we hold. And because a belief is something that we no longer question, it lies just below the surface of our awareness and works at an unconscious level.

Think back to when you first encountered some new information or experience. You would have processed it in your conscious mind with questions and, on reaching a decision, would have entered the meaning into your mental map and, in effect, formed a belief. From then on your subconscious would have automatically steered you in alignment with your belief. Should you have re-encountered the information or experience, your belief would have popped up like a little flag, saying, 'Don't bother thinking all this through again, because you have already formed a belief about it, and in this situation you have decided to respond in *this* way.'

All of this happens in the blink of an eye, and the system works well, except that not all of your beliefs will be empowering and supportive of your moving forward towards what you want in life. Some of your beliefs will probably be quite limiting. Some may not be as relevant today as they were when you formed them. And some will even stop you from acknowledging that you have any limiting beliefs at all.

We acquire our limiting beliefs in many ways – from a negative remark, a bad experience or maybe a painful failure. Any one of these things – as well as countless others – can cause us to form limiting beliefs about our self and our potential.

All limiting beliefs eventually boil down to 'I can't':

- I can't because I've tried and didn't succeed before.
- I can't because I don't think I'm good enough.
- I can't because I don't feel capable.

In truth, very few of our 'I can't's are based on fact. Usually they are based solely on the decisions that we have made or beliefs we have formed and no longer question. The 'I can't's of your life will always be true for you until you question them, drop them and replace them with 'I can', which equals belief in your self and confidence in your ability to succeed.

By using your Life Map to hold and boost the thought 'I can', you build new empowering beliefs that automatically tune you in to the positive frequencies of happiness and abundance. As you build positive beliefs in your self, your beliefs build your motivation. They open the door to possibility and shine a light on opportunity.

Create a beliefs grid

Identify and make a note of some limiting beliefs (LBs) that you are aware of in your self. In your journal draw up a grid, using the example below as a guide. It may help to begin the process by thinking about what you want (your goal) for each area of your life and then identify any limiting beliefs related to that goal. For example, someone whose goal is to be in a totally committed long-term relationship may be limited by having the belief 'I can't be free in a long-term relationship.' This could cause them to be fearful and avoid serious commitment.

Then, to create a balance, write down your current empowering beliefs (EBs) related to each goal to enable you to connect to your 'I can's.

Example

Life Area Relationships	Goal To be in a committed and loving long-term relationship	LBs I can't be free in a long-term relationship	Current EBs I attract men/women into my life

Then fill in the grid for other areas of your life, such as Family, Work/Career, Financial, Recreation, Social, and Community. Once you've started your beliefs grid you can add to it at any time with new goals and fresh insights and beliefs.

Changing Beliefs

There are many ways to change a belief from 'I can't' to 'I can'. Perhaps the simplest, and sometimes the most effective, way is to start questioning it. Ask your self:

- Where did this limiting belief come from in the first place?
- In what ways does it limit me?
- Whose idea was it, mine or someone else's?
- What caused me to decide that this is true for me?
- Does this belief really serve me?

The process of merely questioning a limiting belief is often sufficient to dissipate it.

All of us have a natural ability to collapse limiting beliefs. Children do it all the time. They may believe in the tooth fairy and Father Christmas, or that babies are delivered by storks. And this belief will stick until they discover new information, make new decisions, form new beliefs, update their paradigms and clarify their 'mental map of meaning' to a new level.

. . . .

When a belief no longer serves you it is time to let it go.

. . . .

Some adults carry around with them beliefs that they picked up in childhood – and are not even aware of this. Children will always pick up beliefs from their parents and the other strong influences around them. Sometimes these are great, sometimes they are less than ideal. Because my mother had a very strict and hard childhood, in my adult life I found my self believing that it was not right to take time off or freely spend money on my self. It was only when I questioned this belief that I discovered where it came from.

Many people form a subconscious belief about how much money they should earn a year. If they begin to earn more than they believe they are worth, they often engage in self-sabotage to adjust the figure, but are not consciously aware of what's going wrong. Many psychologists now state that *it is impossible to earn 10 per cent more or less than what you genuinely believe you are worth.*

While our natural process as children is to update our beliefs as and when required, as adults we are generally reluctant to drop any of our long-held beliefs. We form a sense of security and identity from them: 'This is who I am; I'm this sort of person who acts in this way and believes these things.' And that's good, because our beliefs are meant to protect us, to give us a sense of security and identity. However, they can serve us fully only when they are positively focused.

Turn 'I can't' into 'I can'

You now need to add another column to the grid in your journal, as in the example below. For each of the limiting beliefs in your grid, write a new empowering 'I can' belief to replace it. In the example used earlier for relationships, the new empowering belief could be 'I enjoy total freedom within my relationships now.' Ensure each new belief is personal, positive and in the present tense.

Example

Life Area	Goal	Current EBs	New EBs
Relationships	To be in a committed and loving long-term relationship	I attract men/women into my life	I enjoy total fredom within my relationships

. . . .

Sometimes the only way to move forwards is
to let go of the past.

. . . .

You Are Your Beliefs

A friend of my mine, who had a child at sixteen, became conditioned to believe that because of her age she was incapable of being a good mother. It has taken considerable time and courage for her to realize that this belief is based not on fact but on somebody else's opinion.

Another way of seeing your beliefs and paradigms is to imagine that you are painting a self-portrait. Each dab of paint represents one of your beliefs, and together they form a picture of you – a blueprint paradigm of who you believe you are.

The way that you act, the things that you like, the work that you do and the people that you enjoy spending your time with, are all determined by your beliefs. To paraphrase Henry Ford: 'Whether you believe you can, or whether you believe you can't, you're right.'

Fine tune your beliefs

For this exercise you need to copy the seven circles of the mandala opposite into your journal and write the headings into each of the seven circles. Then, from the exercise in Chapter 1 on defining your overall paradigm (page 32), insert your desired paradigm statement into the central circle of the mandala.

Then, taking each circle in turn, ask your self what your current dominant belief is for that area of your life. For example, with 'Mental' the answer could be 'I am intelligent' or 'I am forgetful'. Whatever the truth is for you, write it down in your journal in the following way: 'My "Mental" Belief is ....' Do the same for each life area on the mandala.

Then, working clockwise round the mandala from 'Mental' to 'Spiritual', write in each circle the empowering belief that would most support the achievement of your paradigm. For example, a

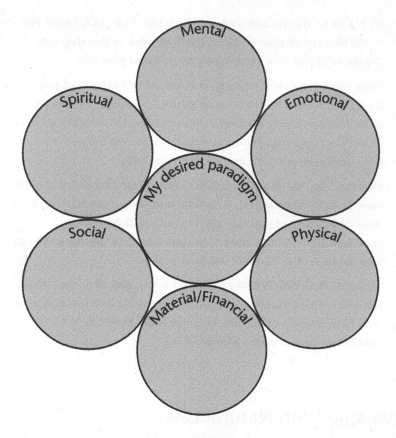

BELIEFS MANDALA

'Mental' belief supporting the paradigm 'Life is a breeze' could be 'I am mentally free.' Once you have done this, double-check that your beliefs are in alignment with your paradigm statement. If not, revise them.

Now sit quietly for ten minutes or so, meditating on your mandala. Allow your self to build a new internal picture of your self. Imagine your self as someone who thinks, believes, acts and behaves in accordance with these beliefs. Get in touch with what it's like to be this person – what it feels like, looks like, tastes like, smells like. Let all your senses come fully alive as you step into the shoes of this new version of your self and your life.

Once you have a clear picture, or sense, of this version of you, repeat out loud seven times your desired paradigm statement, while simultaneously holding a powerful mental snapshot of your vision. Keep repeating the statement and seeing the picture. Now take a deep breath and stretch your body.

Each time you catch your self acting from your past beliefs repeat your desired, empowering paradigm and once more flash up that snapshot picture of you living it. Repeatedly linking your paradigm statement to the picture will reinforce the command to your subconscious to make this your reality.

Trying on new beliefs is like trying on a new pair of shoes – they can feel uncomfortable at first until you get used to them. And, as with new shoes, it takes time to break them in and only continuous wear ensures a good fit.

Working With Natural Law

The laws and principles that govern success are relatively few and simple. They have not in essence changed over time, nor are they dependent on situation or circumstance. Throughout the ages people have sought to understand and explain the forces of nature and laws of creation. Their drive has always been to define and understand the world that surrounds them, to discover meaning and order within the complexity and diversity of life. But in order to understand the wider world, we must first seek to understand our self. Our individual journeys and maps of meaning draw on our left- and right-brain qualities and are a reflection of human beings' progress and collective understanding.

The left-brain qualities represent science and formula, while the right-brain qualities represent wisdom and purpose. The goal in both camps has been to discover the meaning of things, why something is how it is. The left-brain sciences endeavour to arrive at this understanding through theory and equation; right-brain wisdom through experience and principle. Both approaches seek to discover the principles and equations that are the simplest and most fundamental yet explain the greatest amount.

Einstein's equation $E=MC^2$ is actually a very simple formula, but it explains a fantastic amount. Sir Isaac Newton's theory of gravitational pull is also quite basic, but it allows the interaction of the stars and planets to be calculated.

In essence there are but a few fundamental principles explaining the deep truths and wisdom of life. And if we live in harmony with them we are able to flow with the force of life towards the creation of our desires.

Two of the most important principles to understand when working with your Life Map are the law of attraction and the law of cause and effect. These fundamental laws apply to every aspect of life. The law of attraction, at its most basic level, says: Like is attracted to like.

In the human radio analogy, the law of attraction is represented by the aerial which, being two-way, both transmits and receives. This principle states that you attract those people and circumstances that are in harmony with your dominant thoughts and beliefs: As you sow, so shall you reap.

The law of cause and effect has been accepted as a great truth by all people of wisdom throughout the ages and it appears in many different forms.

Fundamental laws are like the wind – extremely powerful but not easy to see directly – and best observed in the movement of the things it touches and its effect.

The Loop of Becoming – Being at Cause

We live in a physical world of cause and effect. The law of cause and effect dictates that nothing happens by accident, that every 'effect' has a specific 'cause'. Applied to ourselves, this law means that the situations and circumstances of our lives are the 'effects' produced or 'caused' by our actions. If we follow the chain back, the ultimate or first 'cause' is our thoughts.

· · · · · · · · · · · ·

Thought is the first creation.

· · · · · · · · · · · ·

Everything that has ever been created began as somebody's thought; every great work of art, every great monument, every great empire, was once just an idea in someone's head.

In like manner, every behaviour and habit that you have, and every emotion that you feel, also began as a thought. Thought triggers and creates emotion. For many people this is a new realization; they have never gone beyond the paradigm of 'If something good happens in my day, then I'm happy, and if something bad happens I'm sad.' And while this may be a personal truth, the ultimate truth is that it's not the thing in itself that makes them happy or sad, but how they think about that thing.

Sit back for a moment now, close your eyes, and focus on something good that has happened to you, either recently or in the past, and within thirty seconds or so your thoughts will begin to trigger the release of the chemicals and endorphins that create the physical feeling of happiness.

Then sit back and focus on something sad and, similarly, within about thirty seconds you'll start to feel sad.

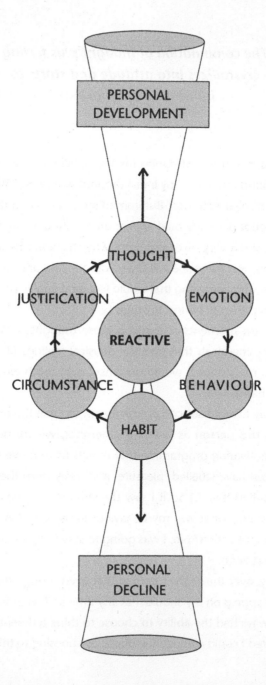

* * * * * * * * * * * *

*The combination of thought plus feeling
crystallizes into attitude and starts to
influence our behaviour.*

* * * * * * * * * * *

I first noticed this in myself during my teens. When I was out and saw someone I found attractive, my initial thought would be, 'She's nice; I'd like to go and speak with her.' But immediately on having this thought, a little self-doubt demon would appear on my shoulder and whisper in my ear, 'Yes, she is very nice, and that's why she won't be interested in you. If you go over there she will blow you out cold and tell you to get lost. Think how embarrassing that would feel. And you've got your mates here watching; they're bound to laugh.'

Within a few moments of thinking those thoughts I would trigger the release of chemicals that give the physical feelings of anxiety and nervousness: my stomach would go tense, my mouth would become dry and my hands wet.

In this way I would subconsciously begin to label the experience of speaking to this person as 'pain'. (Remember, we are born with an automatic motivation programme that directs us to move towards the things that we have labelled 'pleasure' and away from the things that we have labelled 'pain'.) So if I saw the situation of speaking to this person as painful, what was my behaviour likely to be? Would I move forward and take action? No, I was going to stay right where I was, safe in my comfort zone.

Gradually, over the years, I learned that even though the self-doubt demon may appear on my shoulder at any time and whisper to my insecurities, I always had the ability to choose to think differently.

I discovered I could override the doubt by choosing to think thoughts such as: 'I don't think she'd be that nasty, I think she'll be quite nice. And it's not as though I am going to get physically hurt, not as long as I choose my words well and keep my distance. Besides, if she were that rude then she really wouldn't be the type of person I would want to spend any time with anyway. And if my mates laugh – well, they can get lost, because I don't see any of them showing much courage.'

When I think such thoughts I again release chemicals and endorphins, but this time they are those that give me a positive and empowering feeling. And if I'm seeing the situation of speaking to this person as pleasure, then I am likely to move forward.

It doesn't matter whether the particular scenario you face is plucking up the courage to speak to someone you find attractive, picking up the phone to make a call you have been putting off, or presenting your self for an interview, audition or presentation. The way that you think about the situation determines how you feel about it, and in combination your thoughts and feelings influence your behaviour, either spurring you on into action or keeping you rooted to the spot in fear. *But it all begins with your thoughts.*

Any behaviour that we exhibit on a regular basis becomes a habit, and it takes a minimum of ten days to break a habit. Our habits in turn create our circumstances, which we then usually justify and accept.

In the various areas of our lives a cycle of actualization operates. Sometimes it is negative and reactive, pulling us into a downward spiral; at other times it is positive and proactive and the spiral is reversed.

Regardless of the direction of the cycle, the law of cause and effect governs the order of the process and the law of attraction provides the power. A thought triggers off the cycle and the law of attraction enhances the power of each step along the way, building up its force and momentum.

Trying to make changes in your self by working at the point of a behaviour or habit can require a great deal of energy, because by then the thought has grown in power and is rooted in emotion. To change an individual habit, behaviour or your entire cycle from reactive to proactive, from negative to positive, you need to start at the beginning by becoming response-able and consciously choosing to hold thoughts that are focused on what you want.

Every dawn, each man is offered, again, the freedom of choice ... While life remains, there is always the opportunity to remake the world.

JIM COLEMAN

CHAPTER 3

Being at cause

*A man who is master of himself can end a sorrow
as easily as he can invent a pleasure.*

OSCAR WILDE

Response-ability

As a child growing up, I did something that I'm sure a lot of other people have also done: I confused the meaning of the word 'responsibility'. I thought that responsibility meant blame. It is an example of how we place inaccurate labels on our mental map of meaning.

This particular false belief came about partly because of my lack of academic understanding – born out of my inability to read and write – and partly because of the way I was hearing the word. It was usually in the context of, 'BRIAN, are you going to come and take RESPONSIBIL-ITY for this!' It always sounded to me like blame, and my reaction was usually to be on my toes and off away in the opposite direction.

Sangeeta and I have both come across many people who have made responsibility mean duty. In fact, 'blame' and 'duty' tend to be the two most common labels that people place on the word. Interestingly, both produce an experience and feeling of burden and restriction – as if there is no longer any choice in the matter. I call this the 'have to' syndrome.

Years later, after I had learned to read and write properly and had become interested in words and their real meaning, I discovered that 'responsibility' literally means The Ability to Choose Your Response.

We are all Response-Able – *able* to *choose* our *response* to what happens to us. This is our ultimate freedom. Self-actualizing is our divine ability to determine our own path, to become self-determined; it is the power to choose our own way.

⬤ ⬤ ⬤ ⬤ ⬤ ⬤ ⬤ ⬤ ⬤ ⬤ ⬤ ⬤

Becoming fully response-able gives us the
ability to choose Freedom.

⬤ ⬤ ⬤ ⬤ ⬤ ⬤ ⬤ ⬤ ⬤ ⬤ ⬤ ⬤

The Proactive Loop

As explained in the last chapter, the ongoing process of how we actualize our world or circumstances takes the form of a constantly revolving cycle – from the thoughts that we hold through to the cementing of those thoughts in the circumstances and experiences we create. It operates in every area of our lives and can be an upward spiral of growth or a downward spiral of decline. What determines whether the spiral moves us forwards or backwards is our response-ability.

Once we become *response-able* and choose to focus our *thoughts* positively on what we want, our *emotions* start working with us and become *motivating*. There can be no real motivation without emotion. Even some negative emotions (fear, for example) can in some way work for us once our thoughts are genuinely focused on our heartfelt desires.

Now our *behaviour* has *purpose* and *direction*. Yes, we may well be reactive at times while dealing with an emergency, but if our thoughts are focused on our desires we will always quickly get back on track again and continue to take actions that lead to our desired outcomes. In this way, we start to develop *habits* that are *aligned* with the creation of our chosen focus or desires. Our habits create our results and *circumstances*, and these in turn allow us consciously to create and *design* our chosen life. Finally, *justification* becomes feedback and leads to *learning*.

We may not always produce the results that we set out to achieve, but when we understand the cycle of actualization we can act on feedback from our results and *choose* another *response*. By choosing a slightly refined set of thoughts, we create a slightly refined set of feelings, actions and habits – and thereby different results. And we continue to go through this learning process as often as required to produce our desired outcomes.

This whole cycle is part of our natural learning and growing process. Responsibility – the ability to choose our response – means we are totally

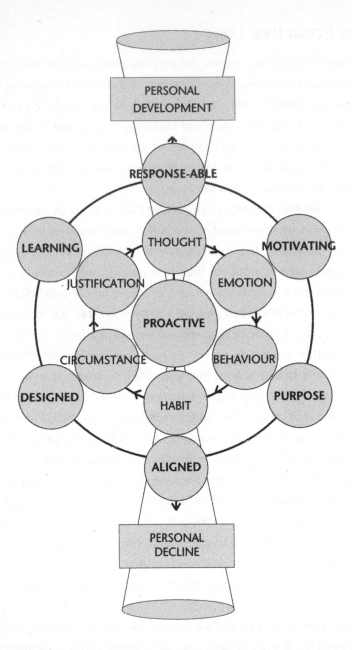

THE PROACTIVE LOOP

free to learn from both our successes and our failures, from both the things that go right and the things that go wrong. It is our ability to choose new thoughts and beliefs, regardless of our circumstances, that enables us to influence the cycle of actualization in a positive way. Thus, through understanding our self a little better and working with the fundamental laws, we can consciously and intentionally evolve our self and improve our lives.

The process of creating your Life Map calls upon you to become fully response-able in this way so you can identify your empowering responses – mentally, emotionally, physically, materially, socially and spiritually. When you live your Life Map your subconscious/automatic pilot becomes conditioned to respond proactively to the situations you encounter on a day-to-day basis.

Natural Learning

Perhaps one of the best places to see these strategies in action is in young children. Some while ago I spent a lot of time with a good friend and her baby daughter. During this period I watched the child progress through the crawling and into the toddling stage.

I would watch her scampering about the room on all fours and moving at quite a pace. I was fascinated by her, and noticed that every so often she would stop and look up at the adults. I tried to imagine what she was thinking. And although I can't be certain, I'm pretty sure it must have been something like 'that two-legged stuff looks pretty good'.

With that innate curiosity we are born with, and the encouragement of her parents, it was only a short while before this little girl applied the first natural learning strategy – mimicry – and decided to try the two-legged stuff for herself.

We are all born with two natural learning strategies – one is to mimic or copy, the other is learning by trial and error.

She would crawl over to the sofa or a chair, pull herself up on to her wobbly little legs and then, automatically, the second strategy – *learning by trial and error* – would begin. She would try to walk, take a step, then fall, but she would almost immediately get up and try again. She would try and fall, try and fall, try and fall until, finally, she stayed up and walked. At no point did she appear to think, 'Oh, stuff that two-legged thing; I'm sticking to all fours.' She just kept on trying until she succeeded.

As adults most of us lose this natural response-ability to learn from our mistakes; instead, we become conditioned to respond to a social paradigm that says failure is something bad that has to be avoided like the plague.

I first noticed this in myself when I was learning to drive. The night before my first driving test I went out with my mates and told them all that I was taking my driving test the next day and would meet them out with my dad's car afterwards. Well, I didn't pass my test, and when I met them out that night and told them I had failed, 'plonker' was the nicest thing they said. The laughter was loud and the emotional pain I felt was intense.

The next time I took my test I did exactly the same thing and told all my friends beforehand. Again I didn't pass. That night in the pub the laughter was louder and my pain even greater. The third time I took my driving test I didn't tell a soul. I didn't want to go through that pain of feeling a failure.

In reality, there is no such thing as failure if we learn from the experience and use that learning to help us move forward. It was putting into practice what I learned from the first two tests that helped me pass the third one.

• • • • • • • • • • •

Being response-able allows us to continue to learn naturally.

• • • • • • • • • • •

The Gift of Failure

When the famous inventor Thomas Edison was endeavouring to perfect his incandescent electric lamp a reporter came to him and said, Mr Edison, you have failed over 5,000 times in your experiments. Will you not now give up this folly? Everyone knows that mankind is meant to light his way by the kerosene lantern!' Edison replied, 'Young man, you do not understand how the world works. I have not failed 5,000 times; I have successfully identified 5,000 ways that will not work, which puts me 5,000 ways closer to the way that it will work.' It took him over 10,000 experiments to come up with the carbon-based filament that remains the foundation of our lighting industry today.

Thomas Edison had a success mind-set. He understood clearly that there is no real failure if you learn from the experience. As he said, 'I am not discouraged, because every wrong attempt discarded is another step forward.'

One of the common mistakes that many people make in their mental map of meaning is that they have a label that reads 'failure is bad and equals pain'. This often translates into 'failure is bad, therefore if I fail I must be a bad person'.

Some people live their entire life unaware that they have mislabelled part of their mental map and have therefore formed a limiting belief that is holding them back in some way. Others continue to refine their mental maps and update them with new and more accurate information, but they progress slowly and do not learn some of the major life lessons until their later years. This is the root of the saying 'Too soon old, too late smart.'

Frequently, by the time most of us have figured out how to get the best from life, we feel as if life has taken the best out of us and we are too tired or weak to try again.

The fast path to success – being able to steer the changes of life towards your desires – is achieved through developing your response-ability to choose consciously your thoughts, feelings and behaviours. This is true self-mastery. It is personal leadership.

• • • • • • • • • • • •

By developing our response-ability we are able to build consciously chosen beliefs and habits.

• • • • • • • • • • • •

Left-Brain Conditioning

The ability of humans to think about their own thoughts, to question their own beliefs and choose their own habits, is generally held to be unique. Most other animals are governed by instinct or conditioned behaviour. This means they are governed more by their left-brain function which operates from memories of what has already happened. In other words, once an animal has developed a habit, it can't consciously choose to change that habit. It can think only about what has been, not what could be.

An elephant is trained by taking it while it is still very young and chaining one of its back legs to a large stake in the ground. The elephant instinctively tries to pull the stake out, but because the animal is small and still relatively weak, it can't. Each time the elephant tries to pull the stake from the ground, a neuron (or brain cell) fires in its head and links up with another neuron and a basic 'I can't' thought gradually forms – in this case, 'I can't pull the stake from the ground!'

The first time this process takes place the 'thought' almost has to force the connection between the brain cells. But the second time the elephant tries to pull the stake from the ground and the neuron fires, the faint path that has already been created makes the connection easier. Subsequently, the harder the elephant tries, the stronger the connection becomes, until the path turns into a road and then a dual carriageway.

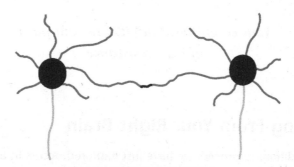

BRAIN CELL CONNECTION

Eventually there comes a point when the neuron connection is the equivalent of a motorway; *it is now the path of least resistance* and has become *conditioned habit and belief.*

When the elephant is fully grown and can uproot entire trees, it is prevented from wandering by a simple piece of chain attached to a small stake in the ground. This is all that is needed because the elephant is *conditioned to believe* that it can't pull the stake from the ground.

One of the most famous experiments in this type of stimulus response conditioning was carried out by Ivan Pavlov on dogs. Every time he fed them he would ring a bell, and after some time he found he had only to ring the bell and the dogs would start to salivate. The outside *stimulus* of the bell would trigger an automatic *response* – the dogs' mouths starting to water.

Years ago people did actually train fleas to perform in flea circuses. Initially they would put it in an upside down jar or glass. The flea would instinctively jump and hit its head, and it did this over and over again. Eventually the neurons linked up and the flea was conditioned to jump just short of the top of the jar. When the jar was removed the flea continued to jump to that same height.

. . . .

***Your conditioned habits are your paths
of least resistance.***

. . . .

Leading From Your Right Brain

The conditioning process we have just explored occurs in all animals, including humans. It is a left-brain process and means that if we allow our self to be governed by our limiting beliefs, past memories and unconscious conditioning, we become like the flea – conditioned to jump only so high, go so far, achieve so much.

But, as humans, we have a unique ability to override our left-brain conditioning and use our right-brain imagination to visualize ourselves becoming something we have never been before, doing something that we have never done before, achieving things that we have never achieved before. Life Mapping capitalizes on this very fact.

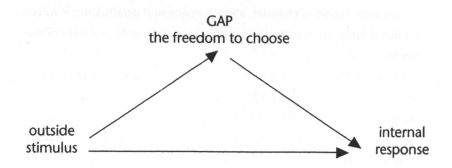

GAP
the freedom to choose

outside
stimulus

internal
response

By exercising our response-ability, we can enter the *gap* between the outside stimulus and our internal response. In this gap lies the freedom to choose our response. This means that at the highest level of thought and feeling we can never be a slave – unless we allow this to happen.

This is certainly not a secret, neither is it rocket science. It is, quite simply, a timeless and fundamental truth! My grandmother knew it well. I can remember her saying to me when I was little, 'Before you lose your temper, my babe, hold your breath, count to ten and think if that is what you really want.'

My grandmother knew there was a choice; I was not so enlightened. My character was such that, right up into my late twenties, I failed to learn that I could choose my response. I remember how, during this period, I was deeply embarrassed about not being able to read and write properly. I kept it a secret for the most part, not wanting even my friends or family to know the true extent of the problem. Every so often one of the few people who knew would make a heart-centred suggestion like, 'Why don't you go and have some lessons; you'd feel so much better about yourself.' This would immediately trigger a fear response in me and I would fly into what I now know as *determinism*.

There are three main types of determinism: *genetic determinism* is in our genes, making us the way we are; *psychic determinism* relates to the way we were raised as children; and *environmental determinism* involves an outside force, such as the Government or a company, that has control over us.

I was using all three without ever consciously knowing what I was doing. At the first mention of trying to learn to read, my fear would propel me into *genetic determinism* to justify my condition: 'I'm dyslexic; that's why I can't read or write. And my dad's dyslexic too; it's a gene thing and I can't do it.'

I would also use *psychic determinism*: 'Oh, I was always moving school when I was younger. I didn't have the same chance as the other kids.' And I would even resort to *environmental determinism*: 'Go back to night school! Are you joking? I haven't got time for that; I've got a business to run.'

• • • • • • • • • • •

In reality, there is no such thing as determinism, only influence.

• • • • • • • • • • •

The truth is that we are all born with strong *genetic* influences, sometimes for better and sometimes for worse. And we all grow up with strong *psychic* influences and are surrounded by strong *environmental* influences. But they are all only *influences*. They can be steered and shaped and sometimes changed completely.

We are each the programmer of our own programme, the creators of our own reality, the authors of our own life. We all, either knowingly or subconsciously, fill in our mental map of meaning. And through response-ability we can choose any meaning for any experience and thereby set our self free.

However, we can only choose a better path if we can look at our lives and our self clearly and create an accurate mental map of meaning. Often the things that are most painful for us to look at in ourselves are those that we find the hardest to see clearly.

How to create a major difference in your life

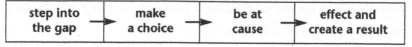

step into the gap	→	make a choice	→	be at cause	→	effect and create a result

The Power to Choose

When I first met my mentor, the man who began teaching me the essence of personal response-ability, I had not long lost my business, my home and my wife. I had a huge feeling of inferiority, a fear of failure and a bit of a chip on my shoulder. After listening to me justify my woes for some time he turned to me one day and said, 'Who is responsible for this sad situation that you find yourself in?' I had a long list of people and institutions whose fault I believed it was. At the top of the list was the Government, which was responsible for the recession; then there were the banks and the brewery who had pulled their loans; then some friends and family members who I thought could have helped more. But nowhere on the list was my name. The thought that I may have made any of the unpleasant things happen in my life was just too painful to contemplate; instead, I found it much easier to blame others.

My mentor said, 'Brian, you have got to bite the bitter pill of responsibility and accept that you have created your reality.'

I struggled against the idea and went into denial, protesting that I could not have done things differently. I would repeatedly use the line, 'It's not my fault.'

My mentor was patient with me and explained several times that he wasn't trying to blame me in any way; he simply wanted to help me understand that at some level I had created my reality – all of it, the good as well as the bad – and that if I could get to the point of accepting this great truth I could also believe that if I didn't like any of it, it was *within my power to change it.* This is what is so fantastic about response-ability. It means *you* have the power.

But, continued my mentor, if I carried on as I was, blaming the external world for my misfortune, I was destined to go on feeling controlled and trapped, like a helpless victim.

For years I played the victim card whenever I felt the need to justify something – the loss of my business, my inability to read and write properly, or simply losing my temper. My conditioning was such that, if anyone did something I considered wrong or didn't live up to my expectations, I would fly into a rage at the drop of a hat and justify my behaviour by saying this person had made me angry. I never once realized that it was me who had set the expectations in the first place and it was me who reacted with anger when they weren't met. It was such a cop-out because nobody can make us angry; rather, we choose to be angry with that person.

* * * * * * * * * * * *

In both minor and very important matters,
our ability to choose is at the heart
of our freedom.

* * * * * * * * * * * *

Choosing Your Meaning

A book that has had a great impact on me and that I'd like to recommend to you is *Man's Search for Meaning* by Victor Frankl. The book tells the true story of how Frankl, an Austrian Jew who was working as a psychiatrist at the outbreak of World War Two, tried to flee the Nazis but was captured and thrown into a concentration camp. He quickly noticed that it was not necessarily the fittest or the smartest people who survived the death camps; more often it was those who had the greatest reason, or meaning, to survive.

Frankl decided that he wanted to survive so that he could tell the world about the atrocities that were taking place in the camps and do his best to make sure they were never committed again. He also knew that he would need to find a way to cope with the pain – not just mentally but also emotionally and physically.

Slowly he began to practise a technique that allowed him to change the meaning that he placed on his experiences. In this way he was able to choose his response at the highest level. He thus attained the ultimate freedom – to choose how to think, and thus how to feel, about whatever happened to him.

We may not always have direct control over our external world, but we are always free to choose how we think and feel. No one can take our inner freedom from us unless we choose to give it anyway.

When I first read Victor Frankl's book I found it incredibly moving. I understood it at a conceptual level and totally agreed with it, but understanding something as an idea and knowing it as an experience in your life are two very different things! The reality for me at that time was far removed from living the principle of choosing my responses in life.

At the time I was working as a keynote speaker for a training company making presentations on motivation. The work involved a lot of driving and the thing that I would get myself most stressed about was traffic.

One day, while hurrying to London for a seminar and just a few minutes into my journey, I joined a continuous line of traffic which seemed to stretch all the way to my destination. By the time I arrived I had completely missed the seminar, I was totally stressed out and in a mood as black as thunder. Later, on the way home, I was thinking about how I had allowed my frustration to spiral and ruin my entire day. To cheer myself up I turned on the car stereo and started listening to a tape by Stephen Covey called *The Seven Habits of Highly Effective People*. I can still clearly remember Covey's words reaching out to me like a personal message, 'If you practise choosing your response on the little things in life, like traffic, it will become easier, and even automatic, to choose on the big things like relationships.'

Steven Covey had a big impact on me that day. I took his advice and soon found that I could work with my imagination to think of reasons to be pleased about the traffic: 'If it wasn't for the traffic, that might be me up in front getting booked for speeding', or 'Great, the traffic gives me an ideal opportunity to listen to some more of those tapes.' Or I could simply choose just to be OK about it.

I genuinely believe that developing my ability to choose my thoughts – and therefore my feelings – has brought me more peace and happiness than I have ever known. In fact, it has rewarded me with much more than I ever imagined possible.

Making choices for my greater good has required me to love, honour, respect and accept my self as never before. This new way of looking at my self, enhanced through the law of attraction, has subsequently drawn more of these qualities into my life and is the true source of the peace and happiness I now experience.

Since those early days when I first began to discover the meaning of response-ability, I have learned that no matter how rich, powerful or gifted we become, every so often we will encounter a situation which we cannot physically control. However, what will always be within our control will be the power to choose the quality of our thoughts.

*The greatest thing that any of us
will ever choose in life
is our attitude towards it.*

In this way we write the next chapter of our story, direct the next act of our play. This is the essence of the ancient wisdom: 'It's not what happens that makes the biggest difference, but how you deal with what happens.' Our response to what happens is the 'cause' that triggers a chain of 'effects'. Always it is our thoughts that we must strive to influence first, for once our emotions have been triggered, physical sensations are enhanced and the law of attraction gets stronger. The drive of the cycle can then become so strong that we cannot influence it.

If you have ever tried to change a habit you will know from experience that the moment you allow your self to begin thinking about the thing you are trying to resist, a spiral of feelings and sensations is triggered that takes you to ever greater levels of craving. Whatever the situation, you must take control of your thinking if you are to have mastery of your self and consequently your life.

*Being in control of your self, rather than
trying to control external events, people,
situations and circumstances,
is self-mastery.*

Choosing Happiness

The mind is its own place,
And in itself,
Can make a Heav'n of Hell,
Or a Hell of Heav'n.

JOHN MILTON

Over many years of teaching this material in large corporate businesses, Sangeeta and I have had numerous experiences of people resisting – sometimes passionately – the fundamental truth that *you can choose to be happy regardless of your situation.* Some people argue that it is just an idea, an ideology, that it's not the real world. The language of these people is normally reactive in nature as they seek to justify their belief.

On one course there was a woman who clearly hated her job, but she was making no effort to find another. Her line of reasoning was, 'Do you really think I want to come to work here, in this tip of a company? There's only one reason I come to work and that's the money. I don't want to come but I have to. I've got no choice; the bills have to be paid.' I asked her what would happen if she didn't go to work. 'Well, I'd have no money!' came the immediate reply. 'And what would that mean?' I asked. 'I wouldn't be able to pay my bills!' she snapped back. 'And?' 'And I'd be in the gutter with no roof over my head.' 'So, what you're saying', I concluded, 'is that you *choose* the experience called work over the experience called gutter. But, understand, you are still making a choice.'

That choice is our freedom. But if you fall into the habit of blaming the world around you for your circumstances you are giving your freedom away and will always feel trapped.

Argue for your weaknesses and they will be yours.

STEPHEN COVEY

Personal Freedom

Any and all of the qualities that create success are within our influence and, therefore, can be our choice. The quality we prize most highly in life is freedom. This quality that we seek, even crave, appears in many forms:

- the freedom to make our own choices and decisions
- the freedom to say yes or no
- the freedom to shape our lives
- the freedom to love, dance, be wild or spontaneous
- the freedom to dream and to realize our dreams
- the freedom to play and to take time off work
- the freedom to engage in all the above, and more, and still feel free inside without feeling guilt, without needing to justify our actions or meet others' expectations of us.

The list is endless, but all our desires for freedom fall into one of the following three categories:
- the freedom to be what we want
- the freedom to do what we want
- the freedom to have what we want

The 'have to' exercise

The more 'have to's we feel we have in life, the more caged and limited we feel and the more freedom we desire.

For those of us who have mislabelled responsibility as something other than our ability to choose our response, our reality and our freedom, the longer and more detailed and regularly used our 'have to' lists will be.

Start by listing your 'have to's in your journal – for example, 'I
have to go to work.' Now take each statement in turn and
consider why it is you 'have to' do that particular thing. Note
how one event leads to another until you arrive at your ultimate
choice. With the above example the process could be as follows:

1   If I don't go to work then I'll be broke.

2   If I'm broke I won't have money to pay the bills.

3   If I can't pay the bills I'll lose my home.

4   If I lose my home I'll have nowhere to live.

5   I'd rather go to work than be homeless.

Notice how your level of personal freedom changes when you say your
final choice. Understand that this freedom is unlocked only by your
becoming fully response-able. *Being responsible* means having the power
always to choose who you are, what you do, what you want and what
your response will be.

· · · · · · · · · · · ·

*Becoming response-able gives you access to
your personal power.*

· · · · · · · · · · · ·

Listen carefully to your choice of words. Make sure you choose those
that build your self-esteem and response-ability. I recommend to people
that they should consider an unusual paradigm of themselves in regard
to work – a paradigm of themselves working *with* ABC Ltd rather than
for them. It is a small change in language, but a major shift in terms of
paradigm and attitude. This is another example of how a little 'fine
tuning' in our self can create great results in our life.

For myself, not only have I made this shift in how I see my relationship to the organizations that employ me, but I have also completely eliminated the use of words that I find uninspiring. Our words are reflections of our thoughts. They have meaning and emotion attached to them. When we use a certain word, it triggers a release of emotion and gives us a feeling, in the same way that a thought does. Sometimes we form feelings towards certain things or situations that could be completely different if we were to change our language.

One word that I have chosen to remove from my personal vocabulary is 'job'. For me this word stands for 'Just Over Broke', where there is always too much month left at the end of the money. Instead I have chosen to replace the word 'job' with 'mission'. I can get excited about the thought of being on a mission. For me it has the ring of purpose and passion. It inspires me to greater effort and activity.

●　●　●　●　●　●　●　●　●　●　●

Being at cause means living your life from the awareness that you are always at some level response-able.

●　●　●　●　●　●　●　●　●　●　●

The belief that I am the creator of my reality now inspires and excites me; it helps me access my power – my ability to change, mould, shape and create my life so that it becomes how I want it to be. The thought that I create my reality fuels me rather than fills me with fear. It drives me forward with a passion that I've never known before – a passion to contribute, make a difference, strive for my own greatness and give of my self and experience for the benefit and betterment of others.

CHAPTER 4

Conditioning your guidance system

I hold it true that thoughts are things;
They're endowed with bodies and breath and wings:
And that we send them forth to fill
The world with good results or ill.
That which we call our secret thought
Speeds forth to earth's remotest spot,
Leaving its blessings or its woes
Like tracks behind it as it goes.
We build our future, thought by thought,
For good or ill, yet know it not.
Yet so the universe was wrought.
Thought is another name for fate;
Choose then thy destiny and wait,
For love brings love and hate brings hate.

HENRY VAN DYKE

Being Conscious

Our entire cycle of actualization – the whole process of steering ourselves towards the things we have labelled 'pleasure' and away from the things we have labelled 'pain' – operates at a completely subconscious level. For the most part, most people will spend most of their life on autopilot, largely unaware of their self, their motives, habits and actions. Sometimes their autopilot steers them towards success, sometimes towards failure.

All of us have an autopilot that helps us move through life. And because it operates through our subconscious mind we are generally oblivious of it unless we consciously choose to focus inwards and become aware of our self. This unique human ability allows us to become aware of our habits, behaviours, feelings and thoughts. It means that we can question ourselves. We can reflect on our thoughts and ask, 'Which of my various ways of being creates my best results and life?' In doing this we can choose to focus on the thoughts, feelings and behaviours that trigger our success mechanism and create not only the results that we desire but, more importantly, the quality of character that we walk with throughout life.

The last chapter discussed how we are all response-able, able to choose the direction of our thoughts. This chapter covers how holding a focus on any thought – positive or negative – begins to programme our subconscious and how, through Life Mapping, we can work with this power and steer our self towards happiness and success.

. . . .

We are free to choose consciously the path or target for our subconscious to follow.

. . . .

The Wonders of Your Subconscious

The subconscious area of your mind, the part of you that acts as the autopilot, is enormously powerful. Even conservative scientific studies estimate that your subconscious mind is around 30,000 times more powerful than your conscious mind. It is your subconscious mind that does the work of getting you through the day, while your conscious mind sets the direction.

Your subconscious works as a helper to your conscious mind. In just seconds it can run complex equations and calculations, such as accurately estimating the speed of an oncoming car as you cross a busy road and how long you have to cover the distance, or tracking the speed and direction of a moving ball as you jump up and effortlessly pluck it from the air. These types of estimations and calculations would take you hours to do consciously, or they may even be beyond your conscious ability altogether.

However, your subconscious mind can do all of this, and much more, all at the same time. It governs all of your automatic systems so that you don't need to think consciously about them. It regulates your heart to beat around 115,200 times a day; it governs your temperature, circulation, respiration and muscle response. Your subconscious is also chief librarian to all of your memories; it observes every thought that you think and permanently records all that is going on around you – both things that you thought you had forgotten and things that you were not even aware that you knew.

People are amazed at how, under hypnosis, when the power of their subconscious is freed, they can remember the name of every person they have sat next to in every class in every school they ever attended. They can remember the smallest details of some of the most seemingly unmemorable things. They can even call up abilities, both mental and physical, that they didn't know they had.

In fact, your subconscious is so powerful that it has abilities to do things that science still can't explain and which most people never even begin to develop or utilize. For example, no one really needs an alarm clock! Have you ever had the experience of needing to be up at a very early hour for something that is so crucial that you set two alarm clocks and arrange an early morning call – and then, just a few moments before all the alarms go off you are suddenly wide awake?

When I was about seven my uncle said to me, 'Brian, if you tap your head seven times, you'll wake up at 7 o'clock in the morning.' I was just a small child, excited at the idea of learning something new, and I believed my uncle without question. I tried it, it worked like magic, and I used this technique for many years.

Much later in my life, when I started to understand how the sub-conscious area of my mind works, I realized the process was achieved by setting a target or goal for my subconscious to follow. I still use the tech-nique today, only now I don't tap my head. Instead, I simply picture the hands of a clock pointing to the time I want to get up, and without fail I wake up within one or two moments of that time. What's more, because my self is being instructed from the inside rather than being 'alarmed' from the outside, I wake up feeling refreshed and much more energetic.

Programme your self from the inside

1 Just before going to sleep, tell your self what time you want to wake up.

2 Close your eyes and picture in your mind the hands of a clock pointing to your chosen time. Then see your self jumping out of bed at exactly that time, feeling refreshed and energetic.

3 Trust your subconscious to carry out the command. The degree to which you believe in your self will determine the degree of accuracy you achieve.

As you begin to have successful experiences, your belief in the technique – and in your self – will grow and your accuracy will improve.

In a similar manner, many people have the experience of going to bed with a problem or question on their mind, then waking up in the morning with the answer.

One of the more common examples of this subconscious function occurs when you are trying to remember someone's name – when it's on the tip of your tongue but you can't quite recall it. Later, usually when you are doing something completely different, your subconscious just floats the name into your mind.

Once you consciously give your subconscious a command, by focusing on what you want you in effect set a goal and your subconscious starts working to achieve it.

> ... the Universe has no choice but to bring you the direct manifestation of your thought about it ... You understand, the creative power is like a genie in a bottle. Your words are its command.

NEALE DONALD WALSH

Your Magical Genie

Not only does your subconscious have untold powers and unique abilities but – and this is the really great news – all of them are specifically designed to serve *you*. Your subconscious has evolved for one reason: to help you flourish in life, achieve wellbeing and attain your desires.

Sadly, because of outdated and flawed theories that were popular at the beginning of the twentieth century, many people have a paradigm that pictures their subconscious as a dark, brooding, negative, even dangerous, place. In truth, your subconscious is neither negative nor positive; it is simply neutral. It is like raw power without direction. It is goal orientated. Like a guided missile system, it's always seeking a target. Twenty-four hours a day non-stop, whether you are awake or asleep, the subconscious part of you is asking, 'What would you like me to do for you now?'

I often find it helps if I ask people to draw an analogy between their subconscious and a *magical genie*. A genie is all-powerful. It can grant your wishes and help make your dreams come true. It is loyal, faithful and obedient. And all you have to do is *command your genie, clearly and precisely*. This is most important, because for all the enormous power of your subconscious genie, there is one essential ability that it does not possess.

• • • • • • • • • • • •

Your subconscious does not have the ability to make value judgements.

• • • • • • • • • • • •

Your subconscious cannot distinguish between good and bad, right and wrong, fact and fiction. It doesn't know the difference between what you desire and what you dread. Like a genie, it can never *of its own volition* decide to give you something. Always you must ask, instruct or command. Giving the commands, making the decisions or setting the goals about what you want remains the responsibility of your conscious mind. Your conscious mind decides and your subconscious mind obeys.

For most of us, consciously commanding our subconscious is easier said than done. This is where Life Mapping comes into its own. With its simple and fun structure you can effectively make and establish your commands.

A Unique Partnership

The conscious and the subconscious work in partnership. The process of consciously choosing or deciding, then subconsciously doing or acting, is the outcome of the natural way in which the human mind has evolved.

Through the whole of our lives we use this process in everything that we do. It is particularly obvious with those things that we do on a regular basis, like going to the shops or driving to work. Have you ever had the experience of making a conscious decision to drive somewhere and then arrived at your destination with hardly any recollection of the journey? This ability to function on autopilot is achieved because your subconscious is given a goal. When you first set out on your journey you briefly think about or picture in your mind where you want to go. This picturing sets the goal and in response your subconscious starts steering you towards it.

Thoughts Are Pictures

Your autopilot is guided by your paradigms. Each thought that you think forms a picture in your mind. Over time the strongest thought pictures become solidified into paradigms. Many people believe that they never visualize because they don't see clear, bright, colourful images. But this doesn't mean that they are not thinking in pictures or imagining.

Make your mouth water

Imagine you have a large juicy lemon and are slowly peeling off the rind and revealing the glistening segments inside. Then bite into the lemon and chew. Imagine the sharp juice hitting your taste buds.

Most people will experience their mouth watering as they think about the lemon. Just picturing it will trigger this physical reaction, which will happen whether they are consciously aware of their visualization or not.

For many people the pictures that flash through their mind are so fleeting, and sometimes at such a high level, that they are often completely unaware of them. However, normally you need only lie back, close your eyes and relax and pictures of your thoughts will start to drift into your awareness.

We always dream in pictures. You may hear words in your dream but the dream itself will be in pictures. Likewise, everybody *thinks* in pictures at some level. These thought pictures, and the casual comments that you make to yourself, become the commands to your subconscious. The strongest pictures or 'thought forms' become the target for your subconscious genie to steer towards as it endeavours to turn them into reality.

Throughout our entire life we create thought pictures of our self and our life that become memories, and thus paradigms. Some of our paradigms are formed through actual experience, others are only imagined – but all become real in our experience of them. Together they form the blueprint for our subconscious genie to follow in any given situation.

For example, when you want to catch a ball you don't have to think through the process in a slow, conscious manner: extend arm, open fingers, grab ball. You simply have the thought that you want to catch the ball.

The moment you picture something you give your subconscious a command to carry out the actions needed to achieve it. In a split second your subconscious searches your paradigm pictures for one that matches your goal then uses it as the blueprint to influence your actions, feelings and thoughts in order to achieve the required result.

Some while ago my brother phoned me asking if I wanted to go on a bike ride. I hadn't ridden a bike for about fifteen years, but within moments of getting on, the experience felt totally familiar and it wasn't long before I was riding the bike on autopilot.

Our paradigm blueprints build over time but, once established, they can be accessed for years to come. Think about learning to drive a car. When you first begin it seems as if there are a million different things to think about. It takes a little while to become *consciously competent*, which means being able to do it but still needing to think consciously about what you are doing. However, once you have been driving for a few weeks you are able to build a stronger picture and you soon begin to move into *unconsciously competent*, meaning you've formed a paradigm blueprint that your subconscious genie follows on autopilot.

. . . .

Learning how to command your genie to follow the blueprints of your choice is essential for any lasting success.

. . . .

Techniques which utilize this process are generally known as Positive Pre-Play. Although there are many variations they all involve *choosing to focus on what you want to achieve prior to taking physical action.*

Positive pre-play exercise

Part 1

Stand with your feet together. Bring your right arm straight up in front of you at shoulder height. Tilt your head and look down your arm. Now, without moving your feet, see how far you can turn to the right. Go as far as is comfortable, still looking down your arm. Make a mental note of a something in the room to mark how far you have turned. Return to the front and lower your arm.

Part 2

Repeat the process, only this time do not physically move. Stay still. Close your eyes and just imagine that you are turning to the right. Just think the thought and a picture will form at some level. See yourself making the movement as you did before, only now it feels so easy and comfortable that you can go much further – at least 1 metre past your previous mark. Hold your focus for a moment. Make a mental note of how far you've turned then return to the front.

Part 3

Now physically do the exercise again. Don't put any more effort into it than you did the first time. Simply raise your right arm, turn, and see how far you can go.

Finally, make a note of this experience in your journal.

You will more than likely discover you can go further the second time. This is because you created a thought picture that became a goal. Your subconscious took this as your command and then worked with you and by relaxing and contracting the various muscles helped you achieve your goal.

Powerful Dominant Thoughts

Top sports people spend an increasing proportion of their training time using visualization techniques such as this to improve their physical performance.

Some years ago my friend and ex-business partner, John, was coaching a sportsman for the high jump. This athlete would run, take his jump and, if he cleared the bar, walk back calmly and unemotionally for another attempt. But if he jumped badly and knocked the bar off, he would lose his temper and expend much emotion on cursing, screaming and generally kicking up a fuss.

Remember, from the moment he starts his run he is on autopilot. Each performance, both the desired and the undesired, is produced from a paradigm. Judging by his behaviour, which thought picture do you think this man was making dominant?

Your genie always selects your dominant thought, and what makes one thought or paradigm more dominant than another is the *emotion* and *repetition* behind it.

· · · · · · · · · · · ·

Adding emotion turbocharges your thoughts.

· · · · · · · · · · · ·

By losing his temper and getting upset, this sportsman was making his undesired performance the dominant paradigm and the one most likely to be selected, thus creating a downward spiral in his performance.

To help him improve, John encouraged him not only to visualize himself clearing the bar before taking his first step, but also to switch his paradigm, feelings and behaviour about his results. When he jumped and knocked the bar off, he was encouraged to say calmly, 'I'm learning and improving.'

When he jumped really well and cleared the bar, he was encouraged to be happy and celebrate the achievement by punching the air and shouting. This process quickly enhanced the desired paradigm and made it the dominant blueprint. Subsequently his performance greatly improved.

Adding Emotion

For everything that we do, in every area of life, this same process is in operation. By adding emotion to a thought we increase its impact on our subconscious and send a powerful command to our genie.

All thoughts carry a varying degree of emotion. For instance, 'I suppose I'll give it a try' is nowhere near as powerful as 'I am definitely going to do it', which carries more emotion and thus creates stronger belief and more determination and certainty. It is obvious which thought will manifest the quicker. The stronger the emotion and the greater the power of the thought, the faster it is actualized.

I once worked with some salespeople who were achieving a good result on all of their small and medium sales but not on their larger opportunities and appointments. Sitting down with these people I asked them to talk me through a typical 'big deal day' and identify what was most on their minds throughout the day, from the moment they awoke in the morning. It soon became obvious that because of the perceived importance of the deal – the prestige and commissions – they were all attaching a great deal of emotion to their thoughts and making them very dominant. They were attaching much more emotion to the big deals than to the small and medium ones, which would have been fine except that the focus of their thoughts was on everything that could go wrong.

And the time that they thought most about this was while driving on autopilot to their presentation. Not surprisingly, by the time they arrived the dominant thought they had programmed their subconscious to follow was of all the things that could go wrong. This was exactly what they were unconsciously steering themselves into more often.

To help them overcome their challenge and improve their perform-ance, I taught them to use the technique of positive pre-play. The first step was to choose an earlier time – such as the day before – to discuss where any potential sticking points might be so that on the day of the presentation they could keep their minds focused on the outcome they wanted.

In particular, I encouraged them to sit for a few moments prior to entering their meeting and, *with feeling*, visualize themselves achieving whatever they wanted to achieve.

The technique works equally well for anyone going for an interview or assessment. Very often people make judgements about you within the first few seconds. In the main, communication is subconsciously transmitted and received in the tonality of your voice, body posture and gestures. If you allow your self to begin picturing the meeting or interview going badly, you can find your self slipping into a downward spiral of anxiety and nervousness which can create a negative impression.

It is not necessary to see all of the detail of what you wish to achieve. Simply picture the end result you desire so your genie knows which paradigm blueprint to use. This does not mean that no physical practice is needed. There must be physical experience and practice to produce a paradigm in the first place. However, by choosing your focus you enhance this picture more and improve.

Steps for positive pre-play

1. Think, picture and state clearly your desired outcome, always asking for the greatest good for all concerned.

2. Stay focused on your desired outcome by repeatedly thinking about or stating it.

3. Visualize the event or experience going well and see yourself achieving your desired result.

4. Add plenty of positive emotion to your visualizations.

What Do You Want?

If you conducted a survey asking 'What do you want out of life?' you would find, maybe to your surprise, that most people don't really tell you. Their answer is usually focused on what they *don't want*:

- They don't want to put up with the same old situation.
- They don't want to worry about the bills.
- They don't want to go without.
- They don't want to be unhappy or fear the future.

The fact is, most people spend most of their time thinking or worrying about what they don't want to happen. And if you consistently think about what you don't want, you create dominant thought pictures or paradigms of what you don't want and your subconscious genie, not being able to make value judgements, simply obeys the pictures because it thinks this is what you do want.

When you do not set a goal for your subconscious genie it decides by default, selecting your dominant thought or phrase as its command. Your subconscious listens to every word that you speak and observes every thought that you think. Whatever your conscious mind decides, your subconscious must obey. Say 'I have a terrible memory' and your subconscious will help you to forget. Repeat the thought 'I can't do it' often enough and your genie will start working to make sure this is true.

Check your self-talk

Listen to your own self-talk as you go about your day. You will find that you become more and more aware of the things you say to your self. As your awareness of your self-talk grows, you can consciously choose the quality of it, changing negative statements and questions into positive ones, as in the examples overleaf.

Negative self-talk	Positive self-talk
I have a terrible memory.	I can improve my memory.
It's not my fault.	I am response-able.
Why do I always get that wrong?	How can I do better next time?
I can't draw.	My drawing is always improving.

Becoming Your Thoughts

What do you imagine successful people think about most of the time? They think about success. They focus on possibility and opportunity. They think about all the reasons why they can and should succeed, and inevitably they spot an opportunity.

In contrast, unsuccessful people think most about what they *don't want*. They focus on lack, limitation, difficulty, and all of the reasons why they can't succeed – the blocks, the barriers. Angry people focus on reasons to be angry, sad people on reasons to be sad. Happy people on the other hand choose to focus on happiness.

The fundamental laws of actualization and creation are the same for both the successful and unsuccessful person; all that is different is what each one chooses to focus on.

• • • • • • • • • • •

*Whatever we focus on we attract
and move towards.*

• • • • • • • • • • •

When my brother was learning to drive I took him out for some extra practice. I remember one occasion when he was steering too close to the kerb. My reaction was to shout, 'Watch the kerb, George,' which only made the situation worse. Startled, he immediately turned his head to focus on the kerb, automatically turning the wheel – and the car – in the direction of his focus, and steered into the kerb.

One of the great challenges in life generally is that it's so easy to fall into the trap of focusing on the negative – the things that we don't want. People find it almost impossible *not* to think about the things that concern them.

Years ago I was owed money by a company for running some workshops. After nine months of waiting for payment and seeing the debt grow ever larger, I started to feel negative and bitter. My base thought and feeling was, 'They don't care about me; I've worked hard for them and they don't care.' While driving into work with a friend I negatively predicted, 'The cheque won't be there again today.' She asked, 'What's your dominant thought on this?'– to which I answered, 'Getting the money of course!' 'No, it's not,' she replied instantly, 'Your dominant thought, Brian, is *not* getting the money. You whinge and whine about it every day. Why don't you focus on the cheque arriving through the letterbox. That's what you want, isn't it?'

The realization was like a slap around the face, allowing me a paradigm shift and some *clarity on reality*. I went straight to my computer and created the biggest dummy version of a cheque that my printer could manage – made out to me for the amount of money outstanding. I printed it out and pinned it up by my desk. Each day it prompted me into visualizing that I already had the money in my possession, and within two weeks the cheque arrived.

The principle that *you create what you focus on* is fundamental and universal. At one level, changing my focus to imagine that I already had the money softened my attitude, which helped improve relations and the money was paid. At another level, through the law of attraction, changing my focus changed my way of being – my vibration – and I drew the money to me.

Ultimately, at whatever level you choose to view your life, it is always a consequence – through the chain of *cause and effect* – of the thoughts that you think.

- - - - - - - - - - -

Think the thought, feel the feeling, influence the action.

- - - - - - - - - - -

You think a thought and then subconsciously take the action. This process can be seen clearly in children. If you give a child a full glass of water and tell him repeatedly not to spill it, he'll try not to wobble but by picturing trying not *to spill the water,* he'll immediately do just that.

On both the smaller things in life, like trying not to spill water, and the bigger life issues, like trying not to mess up meaningful relationships, people unintentionally sabotage opportunities by thinking base thoughts such as 'better not fail this test', 'better not blow this chance', 'better not waste my life'. *We may consciously know what we don't want to happen, but our subconscious genie doesn't.*

Even if we don't go all the way and completely wreck our chances through worry and doubt, such thoughts are enough to limit our power considerably. It's like taking two steps forward and one step back.

Power flows where your focus goes, which means:

- - - - - - - - - - -

Worry is negative goal setting!

- - - - - - - - - - -

Think about it. When you worry you first use your right-brain imagination to create a picture of the worst possible outcome. Then you roll the picture into a loop by thinking about it over and over again and, just to make sure that your worry is your dominant thought for your subconscious genie to act on, you add loads of emotion – such as fear and anxiety. Then, lo and behold, *the very act of thinking about the worst possible outcome* is what selects the paradigm blueprint for its creation.

When I first started making presentations I hadn't learned to hold my focus and would become extremely nervous. I never had any real fear of public speaking itself, but was not confident that I was sufficiently qualified to teach this kind of material. One day I was asked to speak at the very type of place that represented my greatest fear – a university. I can clearly remember pacing up and down outside the seminar room, wringing my hands and thinking to myself, 'I don't want to be nervous. I don't want to be nervous; I really don't want to be nervous.' What was then dominant in my mind was a picture of me being nervous. My subconscious genie read this picture and in effect said, 'Brian spends all his time thinking about *being nervous,* so that must be what he wants. Better make sure he gets it. Call up the paradigm blueprint where Brian mumbles his words, forgets some key point, has a weak tentative voice and fidgets nervously.'

Some of my greatest breakthroughs have most definitely sprung from learning to hold a picture of my desired outcome prior to taking any physical action. I believe this to be the major key to steering change in the direction of your desires, and as such it has become the basis for Living Your Life Map.

This information is not new. In the Bible it states; 'As a man thinketh in his heart, so is he.' And the Buddha said, 'We are what we think. All that we are arises with our thoughts. With our thoughts, we make our world.'

Napoleon Hill, author of *Think and Grow Rich*, after interviewing hundreds of successful people, concluded, 'Whatever the mind can conceive, and believe, it can achieve.' But my favourite quote is by the American philosopher Ralph Waldo Emerson: 'Man is not what he thinks he is, but what he thinks, he is.'

You become what you think about.
You become your dominant thought.

Blind Spots

For years I have been fascinated by how, under the influence of hypnosis, people discover they have all manner of amazing abilities. I am particularly interested in how people in a state of trance can be given a command not to see certain things, and how, after they return to full consciousness, they are completely unaware of what it was they were commanded not to see. The process is known as a *scotoma*, a blind spot blanking something from our awareness.

When we look at something, light-waves are reflected from that object and impact on the retina of our eyes. The retina translates the light-waves into electrical impulses, which travel to the back of the brain. Here they are transformed into a three-dimensional picture of what we *believe* we are seeing.

The old saying 'seeing is believing' is quite literally back to front. *Believing is seeing* would be more accurate. Our eyes pick up only a certain amount of information at any one time, and we constantly fill in the rest with what we *believe* is there.

When someone is hypnotized, the conscious mind becomes sleepy and takes a rest, allowing the hypnotist direct access to the subconscious. Because the subconscious is then open to suggestion, the hypnotist is able to implant beliefs or commands. When the subject comes back to normal consciousness, to the best of his ability he will act out the command even if that means blocking out certain sensory information.

All of us hypnotize our self all of the time.
We do it through the thoughts that we think
and the casual comments that we make.

Self-Suggestion

Does this sound familiar? You put down your car keys, but later when you want to go out you can't find them. Instantly you think, 'I can't see my keys.' Next you repeat aloud, 'I can't see my keys, I can't see my keys.' It's normally at about this point that someone comes along and says, 'There they are,' pointing to your keys that were right in front of you the whole time.

What happens is that the thought 'I can't see my keys' becomes a command. When the thought is repeated out loud, the command grows stronger and your subconscious genie blanks the information you require from your awareness, just like being hypnotized. While this can be extremely irritating when it involves trivial things like losing reading glasses or car keys, on more serious issues it can be even life damaging.

A good friend was made redundant a few years ago and the impact of it affected him deeply. He became bitter and negative, frequently coming out with lines such as: 'Finished, that's me; destined to be unemployed for the rest of my life. There's no work out there for me. I'll never find a decent job again.' He would go on and on about it to anyone who would listen, but essentially the person who heard it most was himself. Gradually he formed a self-hypnotic command to his subconscious which became his paradigm and filter on life. I lost count of how many times, while out together, I saw or heard of an opportunity for decent paid work, but when I would quiz him about it afterwards, he would say, 'What opportunity?' His ears and eyes had picked up the information but he had conditioned himself to be aware only of the lack, limitation and difficulty that he constantly told everyone he was experiencing.

Self-Selection

What's great about this is that you can intentionally condition your subconscious to make you aware of opportunities and possibilities that will help you create your goals.

Once, while on my way to run a workshop, my car broke down at the side of the road with a seized gearbox and I was delivered to my destination by breakdown transport. The next day, one of the delegates on my workshop had his new company car delivered to the facility, and during the lunch break I went with him to take possession of a brand-new convertible. It looked beautiful as it gleamed in the sunlight. I instantly fell in love, made an impulsive decision and declared with certainty, 'I'm having one. Whatever it takes I'm having one.' For the next few weeks, no matter where I looked, I saw that particular make of convertible. It suddenly seemed as if they were everywhere! Of course, in reality, they had always been there. Making the decision to have one with such strong feeling had sent a powerful message to my subconscious genie that read: 'This is important, make me aware of all information concerning this subject.' So, as if by magic, I suddenly see these convertibles everywhere I go.

I expect you may have had a similar experience yourself, if not with a car then maybe with an item of clothing or a holiday destination. Whatever you focus on you become more aware of. If your thoughts are focused on success you will become aware of opportunities for achieving success. If your thoughts are focused on failure, you will become aware of all the reasons why you should give up or not even start.

A Check-Up From the Neck Up

Part 2

I have learned through experience that it's a wise practice to every so often stop, clear my mind and give my self *a check-up from the neck up* to see if I am focused on what I want or what I don't want.

Firstly, I check my self. Is my dominant thought focused on what I *like* about my self or what I *don't like*? Then I check my focus on other people. Am I focused on their *strengths* or *weaknesses*? Next I check the current situation in my life. Am I focused on what is *right* or what is *wrong*?

* * * * * * * * * * * *

Whatever you choose to focus on grows in your awareness of it.

* * * * * * * * * * * *

The above principle is a reflection of the law of attraction. If you focus on what you don't like about certain people you will see more and more of that until you find it almost impossible to be around them at all. However, even if you become aware of what you believe are their limitations but choose to focus on what you admire about them, you will see more of this quality and your appreciation of them will gradually grow.

* * * * * * * * * * * *

Focus on what is good about a person and appreciation becomes love.

* * * * * * * * * * * *

Likewise with your self: the more you focus on what you don't like about your self the more you perpetuate that very thing. If you have ever tried giving up something or breaking a habit, you will have experienced that the very act of trying not to think about the thing puts it into your mind and often results in bringing even more of it into your life.

Don't think of a pink rabbit. Don't think of a pink rabbit. Don't think of a pink rabbit. Don't think of a pink rabbit. Chances are you've just been thinking about a pink rabbit! The only way you can genuinely comply with that command is to think about something else.

Always focus on what is best about your self and strive to enhance it. Some people justify how they are by saying, 'If I don't concentrate on what I don't like about myself, I'll become blind to it and just carry on.' The key to moving your self forward is to find balance in your focus. Become aware of what you want to improve, but don't stare at it. Make sure that your dominant thoughts are for the most part centred on what you want to achieve.

I used to have a quick temper. After becoming clearer about my triggers for *losing it* and some fine-tuning of my beliefs, I discovered that real power came from focusing on 'being' the way that I wanted to be – calm, content and confident, even in the face of hostility or adversity.

Each night before going to sleep I would see myself dealing calmly with difficult situations. Gradually this paradigm became dominant and the one automatically selected to guide my attitude and behaviour.

Through this practice I enhanced my paradigm blueprint for patience and naturally steered my behaviour and ways of being towards it.

Questions for a personal check-up

Focus on self

Am I focused on what's right or what's wrong with me?

Am I focused on what I like about me or what I don't like?

What are my strengths?

What is my dominant thought about myself?

Focus on others

Am I focused on what I believe they can do or what they can't do?

Am I focused on what I admire or what I dislike about them?

Am I focused on their strengths or their weaknesses?

What is my dominant thought about them?

Focus on situations

Am I seeing this situation as an opportunity or a problem?

Am I focused on what works or what doesn't work?

Am I focused on what I like about this situation or what I don't like about it?

What is my dominant thought about this situation?

Holding Your Focus

Developing the ability to hold a positive focus allows you to explore solutions and discover ways forward. Employers in every industry value highly those who can create answers to problems.

Some of the most successful people I have ever worked with have not always been the most physically skilled or technically brilliant. Quite often what made them of great value was their fantastic ability to hold a positive focus, even when everything around them appeared to be negative. Their real asset was being able to salvage something of value from the ashes of defeat.

When are you at your best?

When have you come up with your best ideas, when you were feeling up or down?

When do you do your best work, when you're on a high or a low?

When do you get on best with other people, when you're in a positive or a negative state of mind?

When do you get the most done in the least time with the greatest ease?

'Time flies when you're having fun,' as the saying goes. Deals get done, inspiration is born and answers are discovered when you're able to maintain a positive focus. Even if you currently have some pain or negativity in your life, it will be the base thought of 'I can' that will allow you to have a breakthrough and move forward.

The technique of Life Mapping combines ancient wisdom and modern scientific breakthroughs, tying them together with timeless principles to form a practical tool for helping people to hold their focus on any aspect or quality of their self and to enhance it and thus benefit their life.

CHAPTER 5

THE URGE to BECOME MORE

Intentional be–do–have

Awhile, as wont may be,

self I did claim;

true Self I did not see,

but heard its name.

I, being self confined,

Self did not merit,

till, leaving self behind,

did Self inherit.

JELALUDDIN RUMI (1207–1273)

Higher Ground

Late one night while driving home some years ago I had a sudden flash of insight about a technique for helping people achieve more in life. In a single moment I saw, in one whole picture or pattern, a complete system for conscious creation. I knew I had seen something important and it took me almost a year to translate the detail of this insight into a usable technique, test it in my own life and commit it to paper as a training programme to help others.

The technique, which I call Goal Mapping, mirrors the process of creation. It is multidimensional, can be used to achieve any type of physical goal, target or objective, and has proven hugely successful for thousands of people in many different countries.

However, about three years into teaching the system, and having seen myself and others achieve great things through it, I suddenly had another fundamental realization or paradigm shift. I realized that when you achieve your goal, it is not the physical goal itself that is the highest reward or greatest gift you receive, but who you become in the process. For example, you may set and achieve the physical goal of saving a certain amount of money, or buying a particular possession, but then through unforeseen circumstances the money or the possession is lost. But *who you became as a person* in the process of achieving that goal can never be taken from you.

The highest reward you receive in achieving any goal is the growth that you gain as a person, the quality of character that you enhance and develop along the way.

There is an old adage that says it well: 'Give a man a fish and feed him for a day, or teach a man to fish and he will feed himself for life.' It was this realization, the importance of *self* growth, which gave birth to the Life Mapping process. Life Mapping is the sister technique of Goal Mapping. It is the balance, completion and, in some ways, evolution of physical goal setting, because it is a technique specifically designed to enhance and develop your quality of character, to evolve your 'beingness' and help you become a person who achieves goals.

Life Mapping is a tool to help you hold your focus on *being your best you* so you can achieve Conscious Evolution.

Conscious Self-Evolution

Everything is evolving. Everything is in a state of change. Everything is in the process of becoming something else. Sometimes the changes are fast, sometimes slow, but always and everywhere there is constant and ongoing change.

Heat ice and it melts to become water. Heat the water and it becomes steam. The core substance remains fundamentally the same but its form and energy change. Everything at some level is energy, and energy never dies but simply shifts form; it evolves into something else. This process of transition holds true for everything in nature – water, ice, a plant, a person or a thought. Everything has its own vibration. Everything is on a journey, on a mission to become something else. Even we ourselves were once just stardust and starlight at the centre of a sun.

Driving Forces

The path of nature always moves forward. Nature builds and develops through evolution, by gathering molecules together and organizing them into higher, more sophisticated and complex structures, from the amoeba with its single cell to a zebra with billions of cells. At the very heart of this process lies a collection of fundamental forces that drives evolution ever onwards and upwards. Since the beginning of time these driving forces have been at work. They are present within every aspect and area of nature, whether animal, mineral or vegetable. These driving forces are thus within human beings – within each and every one of us. They form part of the wiring of the human mind. They are the source of our inquiring attitude and the drive behind progress.

- - - - - - - - - - - -

Each of us is naturally driven with an urge to become more.

- - - - - - - - - - - -

From the moment we are born these driving forces are at work; they form the reservoir that feeds the spring in our step and our urge to move forwards.

Very often in the course of our work, Sangeeta and I meet people who believe that they don't want to be rich because money brings its own troubles. Sometimes I meet people who even *fear* being wealthy or having abundance. However, I rarely meet anyone who consciously wants to be worse off than they are right now. In my experience everyone wants to feel they are making progress in some way, that they are better off now than they were last year – not necessarily in terms of financial/material gain, but maybe they have learned a new skill or gained new knowledge. Perhaps they have achieved a qualification, passed a test or developed some aspect of themselves – becoming more patient, caring, understanding, determined, motivated, focused or whatever is most important to them. The detail will be slightly different for everyone, but generally we all want to feel that we are moving forwards and becoming more.

One of the great problems in the Western world and, I believe, the source of much misery, is our tendency to distort this natural feeling of *becoming more* into a paradigm that believes happiness is achieved through *having more* – more money, a bigger house, a faster car, more expensive toys.

I believe it is great to enjoy life, to connect fully and explore the fantastic experiences available. It's great to prosper – to increase our income and improve our quality of life. In fact, if we are to be fully response-able and become our best, it is essential that each of us is able to pay our own way and provide for our self. However, financial/material success on its own will never bring true and lasting happiness. In itself, no amount of money will ease the internal restlessness that people feel, because our natural drive is based on *becoming more,* not on having more. That is why so many people experience feeling great and alive while they are striving to achieve something, but once they have they soon start to feel flat, unsatisfied and restless, as if something were missing from their life.

At the beginning of the last century Abraham Maslow said: 'Man is only truly happy when he feels that he is making progress and becoming more.' And therein lies a vital key that so many people miss.

● ● ● ● ● ● ● ● ● ● ● ●

*Work with the natural flow of evolution
by endeavouring to be more
rather than seeking to do more or have more.*

● ● ● ● ● ● ● ● ● ● ● ●

I know people who have achieved great financial and material success. They have all the toys and everything that a person could possibly want, but they haven't found lasting happiness and peace of mind. There are plenty of financially rich but emotionally poor people in the world.

And at the other extreme I meet many people who are struggling, even in their efforts to make ends meet. They have wired up their brain to believe that happiness comes only with money, and because they don't believe they will ever achieve abundance they feel there is no point in even trying and so give up, often sinking slowly into decline.

What so many people forget is that lasting happiness, peace of mind and abundance are created primarily through *who you are being* rather than *what you are doing* or *having*. *Who you are being* is the biggest part of the game. It is the real power behind what you are *doing*, which results in your *having*. In every area of our lives – with our family, at work or within society as a whole – it is *who we are being* that matters most and makes the greatest difference.

Who's your hero?

Think about someone who is a hero for you, a role model, someone you admire and respect. He or she may be someone you know now or from history, or even just an imaginary being. One of my heroes is Mahatma Gandhi. I admire his commitment to peace, his integrity in living his beliefs, and his ability to inspire and lead. Another is my father, who died when I was only eighteen months old. I've grown to respect him from what I have learned about him: his courage and willingness to take risks as well as his apparent magnetism and sense of humour. In my imagination I also perceive him to be serene, an ability I much admire.

Make a note in your journal of what you admire most about your hero. Make a list of his or her qualities.

Generally, about 80 per cent of what people admire in their hero boils down to qualities of character – kindness, patience, understanding, caring, ambition, generosity, bravery – or that person's way of being. And, regardless of whatever qualities they identify, it is invariably their hero's *way of being* that means more to them than any particular skill. Even when their hero is someone with a great talent, such as a musician or a sports star, it is still the attitude and way of being of that individual that is perceived as his or her real gift and greatest attraction.

We choose our friends and social groups using exactly the same criteria. Even in a club where people come together for a shared interest, groups within groups form, based on like finding like, finding someone who shares similar qualities, values and beliefs.

In the corporate world, more and more it is becoming the policy of companies to recruit personnel for their quality of character – for t*heir way of being* – rather than for their *doing* (skills) or *having* (work experience).

A friend of mine recently attended an interview with a major highstreet health and beauty chain. In the interview all of the hopeful applicants were asked only one major question: 'What are the core qualities that you choose to live your life by?' Once my friend had written down her qualities, which were her chosen way of *being*, they were placed next to a list of core qualities that the company operates its business from, to see if they were in alignment. She was given the position, even though many of the other applicants had better qualifications or appropriate work experience, simply because her desired qualities of character were in harmony with the guiding qualities of the company. More organizations now operate from the paradigm that it is easier to recruit people with the attitude they want and then teach them the skills, rather than the other way round.

Even in the world of sport, where fitness and skill are key, it is the athletes' attitude and focus – who they are *being* – that make the biggest difference to what they are *doing* – their performance – and results in them *having* victory.

A swimmer I know once told me that he lost his last event while still in the changing room. He said, 'On the day of the event I really wasn't feeling good and was still affected by my mother's death a few months earlier. When I looked across the changing room at my main competitor, I had a sudden thought that he was going to win. The self-doubt I felt instantly showed on my face. He also saw it, and the realization dawned that he was confident of winning and I was not. I lost the event even before I touched the water. My confidence never really returned and I haven't competed since.'

Often, even great athletes with amazing skills and abilities fall far short of their potential, and even retire early, because they have not mastered their *way of being* and are therefore unable to utilize their talent to the full when it is most required.

Look within for the qualities you admire in others

Go back to your hero list and look at your answers again. Now try to understand that the only reason you identified those qualities is because they already exist at some level or degree within you. It stands to reason that they must do, otherwise you would have no terms of reference for identifying them.

Every way of being and every quality of character exists within your potential and can therefore be developed at your will.

BRIAN AND SANGEETA MAYNE

The Bicycle and Your Daily Activity

An analogy that I often find useful is to imagine that your work, occupation or whatever you do on a regular basis is a bicycle. Everyone everywhere is riding a bike called 'their daily activity'. The back wheel of your bike represents your technical knowledge, skills and abilities, while the front wheel, because you can steer it, represents your social and interactive people skills.

The bike represents your *doing,* which you use to take you to your *having,* but it is important to understand that it is a human *being* that has to pedal the bike. Some days we pedal with real enthusiasm, a sense of passion, direction and purpose. These are the days when we find our flow, the right line to glide with the curves and contours of our chosen path. Other days it feels as if we are constantly pushing the bike up hill: it weighs double and won't stop wobbling, and we feel lethargic, stressed and depressed and would much rather coast downhill. What makes the difference between the days when we achieve good progress and the days when we don't is not so much the terrain we cover as *who we are being* when we ride. And this is true for every area or aspect of our lives. Whatever we chose to *do* or *have,* real power comes from who we choose to *be.*

· · · · · · · · · · · · ·

What are your ways of being that make the biggest difference in your life?

· · · · · · · · · · · · ·

Choose Your Way of Being

One of the participants in a workshop Sangeeta and I gave said that she was absolutely clear on what she wanted to *have,* which was a career as a professional singer. She described how, having had won all the local competitions, she then decided that what she needed to *do* was attend lots of auditions so that eventually some talent scout would spot her, which would lead to a contract, a manager and the realization of her dream. When she had finished telling me of her plan, I congratulated her on being one of the minority who think out what they want and how to get it. Then I asked her, 'Who will you need to be in all of this?' She didn't understand and so I expanded. 'If you have knocked on twenty doors and heard only "no, not interested, come back tomorrow," will you need to *be* a person who believes in her self 100 per cent so as to keep going? When you are performing will *being confident and passionate* make a difference to the *quality of your voice?* Will *being enthusiastic* give power to your words and touch your audience's heart?'

By the end of the seminar she was absolutely clear on not only what she needed to *do*, but also who she would need to *be* in order to *have* her dream.

I remember when I first started working in sales and wasn't exactly sure how to proceed, I decided to copy what the most successful people in the organization were *doing*. One of them was even open enough to share with me his process and explained that many of the people he went to see say 'no' but that enough say 'yes' to make it all worth while.

Unfortunately, because I hadn't learned to copy this man's beliefs or ways of being, only his actions and behaviour, my presentations lacked the power of passion. Everyone said 'no' and I lacked the belief and confidence in my self to keep going.

The Syntax of Success

Many people make the mistake of not thinking about who they need to *be* as part of their strategy for what to *do* so as to *have*. In the syntax or cycle of success, to be comes first, then you do in order to have. Study people who have achieved anything of value and you will see that not only did they live to the full qualities such as self-belief and confidence but, more importantly, they did so before they had any physical evidence that they would bring success.

Be–Do–Have is an ongoing cycle or loop. Each part triggers and boosts the others. Hence the more we have or achieve as a result of who we are being and what we are doing, the more we become through the experience. In other words, the more experiences we *have*, the more opportunities we are given to learn about our self and grow.

By following the syntax and *be–do–have* sequence of success, we maximize our physical effort and work smarter rather than harder.

Whole-Brain Creation

Conscious creation begins with right-brain imagination and the birth of a vision of intention.

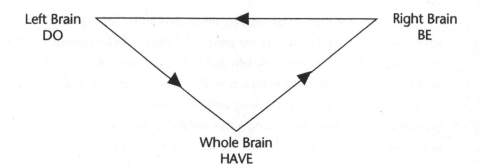

Left Brain
DO

Right Brain
BE

Whole Brain
HAVE

Some people find it a little strange when they first work with the principle of leading their life from their right brain. Often, even the diagram above feels awkward to them because it reads from right to left. This is because, in the Western world at least, although it is not *natural* we have been conditioned and trained to read from left to right. We have been conditioned to rely on our left brain more than our right, and anyone who has achieved true success can be seen to have led their life from right-brain qualities.

Amongst the foremost qualities of your right brain are imagination, emotion and vision, while your left brain has the qualities of logic, order and structure. When in balance, each half complements the other and as a result becomes greater and develops. For instance, it is your right brain that you use to recognize someone's face, but your left to put a name to it.

It is a fantastic system, one that allows us to exercise our free will and create our chosen desires. The moment you engage your right-brain imagination and picture your future, your left-brain logic starts looking for the most effective path or structure that will take you there. Your left brain uses its abilities to identify the best route, utilizing the resources you already have with the most ease. The more balanced both halves of your brain are, the more complementary they become and the greater the resulting synergy.

While there is still great debate over what constitutes 'true genius', what is known for certain is that the people considered to be geniuses are equally brilliant with both their left- and right-brain functions. Mozart could have excelled at mathematics as well as music. Leonardo da Vinci is famous for his structured thinking and inventions as well as for his great works of art. Even his working notes and manuscripts are a mixture of right-brain pictures and left-brain words on the same page.

• • • • • • • • • • • •

Balance creates effectiveness
at any and every level.

• • • • • • • • • • • •

Synergy of Self

Balance is fundamental to success. In anything and everything balance is one of the major keys. There are many areas and aspects of life in which we wish to experience balance, but because they all ultimately evolve according to the law of cause and effect, we need to achieve balance in our thinking first.

Every *way of being* that you develop is most powerful and productive when it is balanced – for instance, when courage is balanced with consideration. Any way of being is just that – *a way of being*. It is neither good nor bad, right nor wrong, just neutral – until, that is, you give it meaning, which in turn determines whether it serves and empowers you or limits and blocks you.

Everyone's balance point is different. To achieve balance in your way of being and hence create synergy of self, you usually need to aim for t*he way of being that serves your greater good.*

We all create our own realities through the thoughts that we think. Therefore becoming balanced in our thinking automatically helps us to achieve balance in our life. Unfortunately, the majority of adults have a degree of imbalance in their thinking in that they are either left- (most of us) or right-brain dominant. Right-brain-dominant people are very creative, forever coming up with new and inspiring ideas, but lack the left-brain logic and discipline to get many of them started, let alone finished. On the other hand, left-brain-dominant people usually fall into the trap of trying to lead their life from logic and left-brain thinking alone. Their 'how to's or strategies come mainly from their past, hence their problem-solving or creative abilities tend to be linear and restrictive.

The left brain operates from memory of what has already happened; it looks backwards to evaluate the present. A person who applies this kind of thinking to life says, 'I need to do *x* amount of work to earn *x* amount of money to pay *x* amount of bills so that I can survive.'

The more dominant the left brain becomes, the greater the tendency to operate from paradigms of the past. Many people fall into the trap of living their life from the left brain. Some have very good jobs and earn very large salaries, but because lifestyles usually rise to match incomes they have equally large mortgages and outgoings, which means they can't afford to stop working or easily choose to do something different. The key to getting off the treadmill is to create balance in your thinking and lead your life from your right brain. The right brain must lead the left brain if you are to define a life and a path for your self.

Your right brain is the source of your *being*; your left brain is the source of your *doing*. The more practised you become at consciously choosing your *being*, the more you empower and support your *doing*, thereby more effectively achieving your chosen *having*.

Very often the work that Sangeeta and I do in our one-on-one coaching sessions, even with some of our top executive clients, involves coaching a person into *being more* and actually *doing less* to create a greater *having* or result.

Who Are You Being?

The practice of consciously choosing your *way of being* is the path to self-mastery. Only a small percentage of the population consciously learn to choose their *way of being* before acting or making a decision – which is probably why so many people have the experience of walking away from various situations saying to themselves, 'I wish I'd *been* a little more ...'

How many times have you looked back on a situation – at home, at work or out socializing – and known that you could have achieved a far better outcome or result if you had *been* a little different in your self?

The ability to choose our way of being happens in the moment – it is a *now* experience. Balance will always be relative to the person or situation *in that moment*. Therefore we must develop our ability to choose in each moment. *Now* is all we truly have and *now* is when we truly create. Every thought you have triggers a cycle of emotion, attitude, behaviour and action that leads to your result. Each cycle begins in a moment of *now*. We are always thinking. In every moment we are consciously or unconsciously producing creative thoughts. Each thought triggers the cycle of creation regardless of whether or not it is what we want, desire or choose.

Therefore, in order to choose your way of being you must become consciously present and aware of your self. Taking total responsibility for consciously choosing your thoughts and your way of being in any given moment leads to self-mastery – and to the natural rewards of owning your true inner power, leading your life from the front and living life to the full.

Who are you being right now?

Write your answer in your journal. For example, as I pause to ask myself this question I am connecting inwardly to my 'beingness' and recognizing that I am being thoughtful, focused, clear, peaceful, passionate, proactive, questioning and committed. It may help to close your eyes the first few times you do this and take your attention within so as to raise your awareness.

Now ask yourself if your way of being is in alignment with your intended outcome. Are you fully aware of your intended outcome. Maybe it's to finish reading this chapter or the book, or maybe it's to understand the importance of the content and how it applies to you so you can use it fully.

Remember, having conscious clarity of intention always allows you to identify who you need to be and what you need to do in order to accomplish that intention.

If you found it quite hard to describe your way of being or maybe struggled for the right words, it's often because you are exercising a new muscle, activating a part of your right brain that you don't normally work with.

Developing this ability takes practice; if you are anything like me you have probably been taught throughout your life to be a human doing not a human being!

If you can master the art of choosing to be present and aware of your way of being in any given moment, you can exercise your freedom to choose the way of being that will best create your intended outcome.

The 'Choose My Way of Being' game

Choose a time when you can devote a whole day to playing this game, and for the entire day practise the art of consciously choosing your way of being in the moment.

Start the day with some mental relaxation and preparation. Close your eyes and take three long, deep, slow breaths. Breathe in through your nose and say to yourself the word 'Relax' as you breathe out through your nose.

Keeping your eyes closed, repeat the words 'I live in the moment called NOW.' Repeat this phrase seven times in all, each time giving the words more meaning and feeling and truly believing them to be true.

Now run through your day ahead at fast speed for a few minutes. Imagine the day going just the way you want it to. See your self approaching every situation with clarity of intention and your chosen way of being. See the day being thoroughly enjoyable and successful for all concerned.

When you have finished say the words 'May what happens be for the greater good of all,' and gently take another three deep breaths as you start to become aware of your self and your surroundings again. Open your eyes on the third breath and stretch your arms up to the ceiling and push your feet firmly into the ground to ensure you are fully back in the present moment.

Make 'Who am I being?' your dominant thought and question for the day. Repeat 'Who am I being?' to your self as many times as you can.

With every experience, person, event and situation you encounter – from the moment you awake to the moment you go to bed – practise the art of becoming aware of your way of being by asking your self this question.

Choose a different way of being if the one you have is not in alignment with your intended outcome.

Here are some other questions for the be–do–have cycle that might help:

1   What do I intend to create now?

2   Who do I need to be in order to create this outcome?

3   What do I need to do in order to create this outcome?

Remember, always choose an intention that is clear and that will serve your greatest good. In other words, what intention would most support you in creating peace of mind, happiness and abundance?

Before the end of the day take some time to write about your experiences. Make a note in your journal of what might have changed for you during the day, what worked about playing this game, what didn't work and what was missing for you.

In time and with practice you will find that in most situations you are quickly and automatically able to get into the habit of choosing your way of being. You will be empowered by the level of clarity, objectivity and responsibility you bring to the quality of your thinking, your ways of being, your attitudes and your behaviours, which in turn will influence your results.

Very often I work with people who know the outcome they desire and are taking some form of action towards it, but owing to a distorted belief their way of being is negative or out of alignment with what they want and therefore the power of their *doing* is greatly diminished.

We are only truly powerful when our *beingness* is in alignment and harmony with our *doing* and desired *having*. Those who work with the positive energy of enthusiasm will always be more powerful than those who merely take physical action.

Great people are not born great; they achieve greatness by reaching out, stretching for their best and moving towards their dream.

Choose to be great. Choose a quality of greatness to live by each day. Think again about your personal hero and choose one quality of character that you identify with greatness. Choose to focus on being that quality to the best of your ability for one whole day. Experience the difference that it makes. Then each day choose a new quality and strive to live at a new level.

Aim to be *your best*, not necessarily *the best*. Compete against your self and co-operate with others. By endeavouring to *be* your best, you will automatically *do* your best, which will naturally lead you to *have* your best results.

Conviction of the Heart
There's a whole other life,
waiting to be lived when
One day we're brave enough
To talk with conviction of the heart.

FROM THE SONG 'CONVICTION OF THE HEART'
KENNY LOGGINS AND GUY THOMAS

Part II

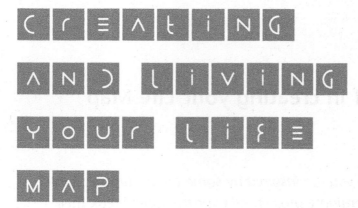

Creating and Living Your Life Map

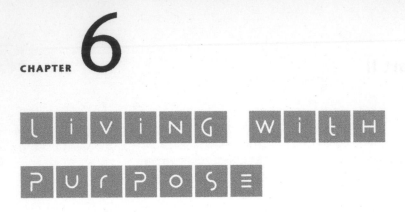

CHAPTER 6

Living with Purpose

Step 1 in creating your Life Map

When you are inspired by some great purpose, some extraordinary project, all your thoughts break their bonds; your mind transcends limitations, your consciousness expands in every direction, and you find yourself in a new, great and wonderful world.

Dormant forces, faculties and talents become alive, and you discover you are a greater person by far than you ever dreamed yourself to be.

PATANJALI, C. 2ND CENTURY BC

Life Mapping

The Life Mapping technique is a powerful tool to help you set and hold intentions as beacons or targets for your subconscious to steer towards on your journey through life. What makes Life Mapping unique and helps create its power is its combination of left-brain statements or affirmations and right-brain symbols or visualizations. Together they form an extremely effective whole-brain system rooted in ancient wisdom and fundamental principles.

Over thousands of years all types of intention-setting or goal-achievement systems have shared the same basic root. Their effectiveness stems directly from their ability to connect your consciously chosen desires to your subconscious autopilot so that you naturally begin to move towards your desires, to create them or, as in Life Mapping, to *become* them.

One of the problems for the majority of the population in recent times has been that they are left-brain dominant and accustomed to thinking mainly in words. In this way they perpetuate left-brain dominance. In addition, many of the 'success systems' that have been available for helping people to achieve their intentions have also been left-brain orientated, often centring solely on using words and statements.

Achievement techniques that function solely through left-brain affirmations can be beneficial, but they are by no means the most powerful approach. In recent years science has clearly established what ancient cultures have always maintained – that the major pathway to the subconscious is through the emotional right brain, which thinks in pictures. This ancient truth can be seen in the imagery of many cultures, from pagan sand paintings and rock drawings through to Christian stained-glass windows and the symbols used in Islamic art. It has been studied by modern psychologists and we even observe it ourselves in our dreams and imaginings.

Through the physical process of creating your own Life Map you activate both your left and right brain and produce a powerful whole-brain connection with your subconscious. The process of changing any of your ways of being, habit patterns, attitudes, deep-seated feelings or paradigms of life can be likened to the firing of a rocket – maximum focus and thrust are needed to power it through the early stages so that it can break free of the Earth's gravitational pull. In like manner, when we seek to make a conscious change in our self, intense focus and concentrated energy is needed to help us break free of the gravity of our old ways of being and stick to our chosen new ones.

The initial power that you produce when you create your Life Map is the equivalent of a booster rocket. It helps you to achieve a quantum leap of progress in your self. Through your continued focus your new Life Map begins to acquire its own gravity and, with your commands becoming the main force, it draws you towards the blueprint for being your best you.

Your Life Map

There are seven areas or aspects of Life Mapping, representing seven areas or aspects of your life. Collectively the areas form a 'mandala', which in ancient cultures signifies wholeness or oneness. It represents 'individuation', the process of coming to an inner unity and harmony.

The centre space of your Life Map mandala is for your purpose, and around the outside are spaces for the mental, emotional, physical, material, social and spiritual aspects of your life. Your completed Life Map reflects you as being *whole* and is a powerful tool to heal any imbalances in your self. As you achieve a greater balance, so you create 'synergy of self' – the whole of *you* becomes more and evolves your self to a higher level of being.

In completing your Life Map you clearly communicate your intentions of your self to your subconscious and your Life Map forms a succinct template of your best you – a simple but profound blueprint for your truest potential, a self-portrait of your magnificence. In essence, your Life Map represents the grandest version of you – your *true self*.

Step 1 in creating your Life Map (covered in this chapter) is to identify and state your purpose in the form of an affirmation – positive, personal and in the present tense.

Step 2 is to identify who you choose to become and the qualities of character you would most like to develop in each of the life areas and then create affirmations so as to achieve your purpose (see Chapter 7).

Step 3 is to complete your Life Map by stating again your purpose and supporting qualities, only this time in a right-brain format by creating a series of symbols or pictures that bring balance to your left-brain statements (see Chapter 8).

Together these three steps produce a whole-brain 'dominant thought form' and create a deep subconscious connection. Your journey begins by exploring the power of discovering and living *your* purpose.

Hype or Help?

When I first started out as a trainer I was given a huge boost by gaining a position with a motivation-based training company in London. I now look back on that whole period and see how it was my apprenticeship into the world of training and development. My daily activity centred on delivering one-hour 'overview presentations' focused on the subject of motivation. I would give my presentation to all types of organizations and seek to attract people to our main three-day showcase seminar.

Very often, the manager of the team or department that I was about to speak to would introduce me as 'The Motivational Speaker'. Right from the start I never felt completely comfortable with that title – there was something about it that didn't seem to fit. However, that aside, I quickly discovered that I was popular with my audience, and I received plenty of bookings. Most people seemed very upbeat and enthusiastic about my presentation and message. Some even claimed they felt 'motivated'.

My challenge began when one day I raised my awareness and, after my subsequent paradigm shift, realized that when I went out the door, for most of my audience motivation went out the window. Maybe for some it would last a bit longer but, generally speaking, the motivational effect I had on people was short lived. This really bothered me, because my genuine goal and mission was to help people move forward in their lives. Make no mistake, I was certainly pleased that the audience enjoyed my presentation, but more and more I began to wonder how much real benefit I was providing.

I decided I must find a way to help people achieve long-term motivation, otherwise there was no point in my continuing and I should look for something else to do with my life. So I committed myself to study the subject of motivation in great depth. I read only on that topic, devouring every book I could find on it. I spoke to all the experts available to me and I studied hard; at the end of one year of focused thought I came to the conclusion that:

• • • • • • • • • • •

The only true motivation is self-motivation.

• • • • • • • • • • •

Self-Motivation

We each enter the world with two natural self-motivation strategies: one is focused on moving us away from pain, the other moves us towards pleasure. Both are designed to serve us. And we use both strategies at different times and in different areas of our life. However, one of these strategies normally becomes dominant. Many people are aware of this at some level and use a combination of strategies – incentives and threats, pain and pleasure – in order to get others to co-operate with them. In reality, this approach has a very limited effect. Incentives (in the form of rewards) and threats (in some form of punishment) have for long been used by people in their attempts to control others. Experience has shown that, at best, the effectiveness of this approach is short term and uncertain.

True motivation can be generated only from within. We achieve this by attaching either pain or pleasure to the things we are doing, or not doing, in order to get our self into action. *We place our 'emotion' to create our 'motivation'.* However, it seldom works well when 'done' to others. Firstly, this is because the match between the incentives and threats must be in alignment with their preference for pain or pleasure, otherwise it will have no *meaning* or *purpose* for them. Using threats on someone who is motivated to move towards pleasure will create only more resistance, de-motivation and even resentment. Likewise, using pleasure to motivate someone who responds more to pain will not work either.

Secondly, and perhaps most importantly, by their very nature these approaches to motivation are 'manipulative' and must be enforced. So when the incentives and threats cease, so too does the motivation.

· · · · · · · · · · · ·

The essence of motivation is a feeling of genuinely desiring to do something.

· · · · · · · · · · · ·

To be motivated, most people have to act of their own accord. Constantly needing someone present to apply incentives or threats would constitute a self-defeating process.

Natural Motivation

True motivation is the process of feeling genuinely excited and enthusiastic about whatever you are doing or intending to do, and then getting on and doing it.

As I gained this greater awareness about the qualities of true motivation, a new question came up: 'Where does "true motivation" come from – what births it?' I found the answer right in front of me, in the people I admired. If you look at people who are 'inspired' you will see that they have a spring in their step and a sparkle in their eye. They have a *way of being* and an energy that other people find attractive and are drawn to. They are 'naturally motivated'.

• • • • • • • • • • •

Self-motivation springs from inspiration.

• • • • • • • • • • •

Inspired people do not need to get themselves motivated – their motivation is a natural product of their *inspiration*. But, sadly, these people are in the minority. For every one truly inspired person there are many others who are attracted to this individual in the hope that they too will become inspired. And sometimes they are. All sorts of people have inspired others, in every generation and in every aspect and area of life. However, true and lasting inspiration is a *Do It Your Self* game. When you receive inspiration from another it is like receiving the spark that lights the fire, but in order for it to become a burning passion you must feed the flames yourself.

Once again, on my search for the roots of true motivation my question was: 'Where does inspiration come from?' The answer I discovered was 'meaning and purpose'.

Talk to people who are inspired about anything, and they will tell you clearly why they are inspired. They will instantly be able to connect with the feelings of commitment and passion that they feel for whatever they believe in and are prepared to make a stand for. Study the people who have shaped history and you will discover that there was a compelling purpose behind what they were doing. They were connected to strong emotional reasons that powered them to achieve great things.

A Sense of Purpose

. . . .

*The more meaning and purpose
you find for your self,
the more inspired you will be in your life
and the more motivated you will feel
through your day.*

. . . .

Inspired people are invariably *on purpose* – on the pursuit of their dream. They are 'on a mission' to achieve their vision.

There are as many different types of missions and visions as there are definitions of success. Some people's purpose and mission will be centred on the achievement of something physical – winning, buying or building something – which in effect amounts to *having*. Others' will be centred on their work, project or career – or what they are *doing*. Our prime or first purpose, however, is always who we are *being*.

Every thing has a purpose, a reason for being. For every living organism the prime purpose is to live and to continue living. The pulse of life shows itself in many forms – two of the most fundamental being the urge to reproduce and the urge to become more, representing the instinct to move forward and grow.

Human beings are also a part of nature. We too have a prime purpose akin to the Pulse of Life – to be our best; to be all that we desire to be; to flourish, thrive, bloom, prosper, grow and multiply.

Sometimes we must push against the elements and at times we come into being or take root in harsh environments, but always our natural birthright and prime purpose is to make the most of our self and our life.

In animals prime purpose flows through instinct. But, as human beings, we have the ability to go beyond instinct and shape our prime purpose of being through our imagination and by defining our vision. We can choose both our own way – our vision – and *who* we choose to become in order to follow it. The combination of our prime purpose – the desire to be our best – and our chosen vision for our future creates our overall *life purpose.*

Having free will means that we can then steer the life-pulse urge to become more and use it as the force to carry us towards our heartfelt desires and dreams.

We are human *beings* first and foremost. To *be*, then to *do* and *have* is part of our very essence. In like manner, our prime purpose or *beingness* is the starting place for discovering our overall life purpose.

Redefine how you see your self

How you see your purpose depends on the paradigm that you are looking through, which is a reflection of how you see your self.

This exercise offers an alternative paradigm for the way you see and describe your self.

Firstly, think of how you would usually introduce your self to someone new. Write what you would say in your journal before going further. For example, 'Hi, I'm ...'

When I meet new people and get into conversation, I often find that on asking them to tell me a little about themselves, not many actually do. Few people describe their self, as in their beingness, to me. Instead they tell me about their doing or having: for example, 'I'm the owner of ...' Or they describe themselves through their profession: 'I'm a ... and I work for ... organization.'

Only a very few people say something about their beingness, their quality of character, such as: 'I'm an outgoing type of person.'

Now think of a sentence to introduce your self in alignment with your desired paradigm, describing your self as your best beingness – The Gift of You. Write this in your journal, too.

I recently heard a friend introduce her self by saying: 'Hi, my name's Val and I'm in love with life!' For me, this description speaks loudly of Val, what she stands for, her essence. It describes her joy, freedom and happiness about being 100 per cent alive.

You will always describe your self according to your own paradigm in the form of Be, Do or Have. *Be* is focused on the roles you play in life, such as parent, worker, etc; *Do* is centred on your physical activities; and *Have* covers your possessions, qualifications and achievements.

Your greatest power will come from a paradigm that takes the essence of all three aspects and follows the 'syntax of success' by having 'being' as its foundation. In this way, your prime purpose of *being* will empower your *doing* and missions and lead you to *have* your visions and dreams.

Each person is unique, with a unique thumbprint and a unique life formed from a rich array of different experiences. No one else on the planet has exactly the same life as you have, because no one else has interacted with all of the same people, had all of the same experiences, thought the same thoughts and developed the same character.

Each of us is a gift, individually and uniquely wrapped. Our gift is our beingness, the way that we touch others. We may believe that we all come from the same place and even go back to the same place when we die, but *who we are being* while we are here in this existence is our prime purpose. Everywhere that you go, everyone that you meet and everything that you do, will be touched by your beingness. It's how you share your self with life. It's like spreading your intangible stardust, which is unique to you and all yours to sprinkle.

Recognize The Gift of You

If you cannot see your own gift it will be because of your paradigm of your self, not because your stardust doesn't exist. Of course this is just 'your' paradigm of your self. Others around you can see your gift because they experience it when they are with you.

This exercise will help you gain clarity. Firstly, give your self permission to see through fresh eyes. This is necessary if you are to embrace fully a new paradigm of The Gift of You.

Choose ten people in different areas of your life that you trust and hold in high regard. Include both males and females, of various ages, and from different backgrounds and life areas (past and present). For example, you could pick your partner, your child, an old school friend, a work colleague, a mentor, etc... List the then names in your journal.

Then, over a period of a week, arrange to communicate with each person, preferably face to face or on the phone. Avoid using e-mail unless it is absolutely necessary.

It is really important that you set the context of this exercise with your self and with all the people on your list. If you want others to be willing, honest, open and giving about what they see as your stardust, you will need to 'be' this way your self.

Your goal is to get them to go beyond any surface paradigms they may hold of you and dive into their hearts to access what they truly feel is The Gift of You. This will take courage, because it means letting down any masks and speaking with honesty and openness to each other.

Tell them clearly why you are asking for their help, what it means to you, and your reason for doing this exercise.

Let them feel your authenticity – the Real You. The more you risk being the authentic you (letting down your masks), the more authentic they will be in their answers.

Use the following questions as guidelines; however, it is important to ask them in your own words.

What is unique and special about me for you?

What is best about me being in your life?

What do you see as The Gift of Me?

What do you love about me?

Once you have asked your question(s), remember to be quiet and listen carefully. Refrain from jumping in; instead, allow your self to absorb with your entire being what you are hearing.

At the end of each conversation make a note in your journal of the key words and qualities that were used to describe you. When you have spoken to all ten, take a look back over your answers, reconnect to each conversation and identify the five qualities that were most frequently cited. In other words, what did you hear most often? Make a separate list of these qualities in your journal.

You will probably find that several words were regularly used to describe you and your gift. Most people who do this exercise find that while they can relate to most of the views expressed about them, one or two come as a surprise and cause something of a paradigm shift. If this happens for you, take some time out to reflect and fully acknowledge this part of your gift. Look back at past experiences for evidence of your being this way, and truly embrace this new truth about your self.

Now begin to give form to your stardust by writing in your journal an affirmation statement using the words that you feel most describe The Gift of YOU – in ten words or fewer. And remember, an affirmation is always positive and written in the first person singular and the present tense.

By raising your awareness of your stardust, knowing Your Gift, you can intentionally give more of this new power to all of your life. *Who you are* makes the biggest difference, and *knowing* your gift means knowing your best you. All that remains to enhance your life is choosing to be *this best you* on a more regular basis. Give your gift to get what you want. Be your best you to create your best life.

The Desire For Purpose

Many people struggle to identify their purpose in terms of their true self or beingness. Sometimes, because of left-brain dominance, it is difficult to see beyond daily concerns, pleasures or activities. For those who do give their future or purpose much thought, it is normally in the form of tangible goals or objectives. But setting goals and having purpose are different. Goals usually have a deadline; they have structure and strategy and are quantifiable and measurable. *Purpose*, on the other hand, is ongoing and a way of being – sometimes a bearing, a direction or a vision, but not an end destination.

Targets, objectives and goals are like stepping-stones or milestones leading to your purpose. They are a function of your left brain and represent strategy and mission, whereas life-purpose, the combination of your beingness and your chosen vision, can be seen only through your right or whole brain.

On your journey to develop your self, to raise your awareness and evolve your beingness to a higher level, it is inevitable that every so often your paradigm – and subsequently your goals and vision for your future – will shift. However, regardless of any change in your vision or mission or how you give The Gift of You, your prime purpose – *growing* the Gift and developing your self as a person – always remains constant. In whatever you choose to do or pursue, your prime purpose always centres on being *your* best, being your true self – your authentic best you.

Feeling genuinely confident that you can let down any mask and *be your true self* as often as possible in everything you do is your *prime purpose*. It is the 'personal prime directive' that is written into your genes, the essence of evolution that with the power of instinct whispers '*be all that you can be*'. *Be* the best you and you will automatically *do* your best and *have* the best results.

One of the major life lessons to learn in order to achieve true and lasting success is to focus on pursuing your prime purpose of *becoming more* as a prerequisite to *having more*. This naturally enhances your life, because by consciously choosing your highest response, choosing *who you are being*, you empower your *doing* and improve your *having*. Choosing prime purpose, in any given moment, naturally helps you to become your *true self*, to step into the flow and, through the law of attraction, allow more magical moments to manifest in your life.

By building your beingness towards your *true self*, you cultivate more of these magical moments, which in turn become magical hours, days and weeks and grow into a magical life.

• • • • • • • • • • • •

Living your prime purpose – being your best you – naturally leads you to do and create your best.

• • • • • • • • • • •

The more you pursue your prime purpose, the more clarity you will gain about your self and life, because every time you raise your awareness you will learn another life lesson and evolve your paradigm. Therefore, the greater your awareness of your self, the greater your effectiveness in achieving true success.

Programmed to Find Purpose

Tony Wilson, a good friend, says, 'There are only two real states in nature: green and growing or ripe and rotten.' Which state are you in terms of your attitude to life? Choose green and growing. Choose your prime purpose of being your best you.

Your evolutionary path to *true self* will, in some way and at some point, be to *know* your self as your best – free, authentically powerful and able to choose your response to your environment.

Experiencing and learning to choose these qualities are steps on the path to self-mastery – to *knowing* at ever greater levels that you are creating your own reality and have free will to choose to be the 'Conscious Creator' of that reality.

Gradually, over the ages, societies have given their members greater individual choice, enabling them to become more confident in taking a stand for what they desire. This in turn has led to greater self-esteem and freedom, manifested both internally and externally. This upward spiral has continued and increasing numbers of people are now designing, creating and living the life of their choice. As sentient beings, we need to have this sense of meaning and purpose in our life. It is programmed into our genes and runs through to our very core.

At the end of the nineteenth century, Abraham Maslow stated in his *Hierarchy of Needs* that: 'After we have secured food, shelter and clothing, we naturally seek to define greater and greater levels of meaning and purpose.'

So strong is our need for a sense of purpose that, if we feel it is lacking, we will go to great lengths to attain one. It's one of the prime reasons why people leave one company, club, tribe or religion and search for another to become part of.

Greater freedom in every area and aspect of life means that although the basic needs of more people are being met, these same people are sensing a greater need to find purpose.

Sangeeta and I increasingly meet people in our seminars who cite 'discovering my purpose' as one of their main objectives for attending. Some have achieved food, shelter and clothing in abundance, but are not happy and feel that there is something missing, that their life lacks meaning. Many of these people have spent much of their lives chasing after more and more material things but have not found lasting, true fulfilment. They have not learned the following important life lesson.

• • • • • • • • • • • •

Without a sense of purpose, all material
success becomes meaningless.

• • • • • • • • • • • •

Purpose Serves

In his bestselling book *Psycho Cybernetics*, author Maxwell Maltz states: 'Emotionally we are designed very much like a bicycle, in that if we are not moving towards something in our lives we lose our equilibrium or balance, and emotionally fall over.'

The path of life will always contain rocky patches – there will be challenges to overcome and battles to be won no matter how rich, intelligent or gifted we may be or become. Overcoming challenges is part of learning through life experience.

If you have a strong sense of vision in your life, the momentum will help you move through even the most difficult of times, obstacles or experiences. Without a sense of purpose, the smallest upset or pebble of discord is sufficient to send you spinning off-balance into disharmony and decline. Without goals, purpose and vision we are rudderless. Like a cork on the ocean we are thrown about by the waves and swept along by the currents.

Over two thousand years ago Solomon said: 'When the people lack vision they perish.' This ancient truth is timeless. And, just as a collective vision and purpose has moved mountains, manifested miracles and founded nations, so can an individual sense of purpose and vision work wonders and create dreams.

Pour on the Passion and Power

The greater the depth of feeling that we gain about our purpose, the greater the degree of power we access to help create it. We all have a prime purpose of being our best, to grow and spread our unique stardust – and in doing so we are all free to leave a legacy.

Choosing to leave a legacy means choosing how we want to be remembered. Some people's legacy is a physical asset – the empire they have founded, a business they have built up or a property they have acquired. Others are remembered for their actions – helping their community to achieve something, correcting a corrupt system, changing a negative attitude or supporting a worthy cause. For yet others the legacy they choose is being the best mother, father, brother, sister or friend that they can be.

In every case, the greater the passion felt, the greater the power to achieve the purpose and the more extraordinary the legacy. This is true not only for those whose legacy is obvious and directly touches the lives of thousands (people such as Nelson Mandela, Mahatma Gandhi, Mother Teresa and Malcolm X), but also for those whose deeds are largely unsung (such as the countless people who care passionately about others and consciously dedicate their self towards making a difference in others' lives).

We can all make a stand for what we believe in and thus make a difference. Even those who have had the worst possible start in life can find some value or meaning in their experience and benefit from it by finding their own way and sharing their success. They are the people – perhaps a parent, healer, teacher or lover – who go the extra mile and make a lasting impression on us. They are the people whom we remember for many years. They are the people who shape and influence our lives by reaching out and touching us. And each of *us* can be one of these people to others. It is our *choice*.

Get clear

Before moving to the next step in identifying your life purpose, revisit your statement describing The Gift of You (see page 134).

Does your statement still capture your Gift and represent you being your best? If it does then restate it as your prime purpose, but if you now have fresh insights, amend your statement accordingly and note it in your journal.

Clarify Your Vision for the Future

The next stage in finding your overall life purpose is to clarify your vision for your future. Lasting success is achieved by first creating the foundations of your life inwardly – by choosing 'being your best' as your prime purpose – and then focusing outwardly by seeking to create a life that reflects this. There are no short cuts to long-term success. No matter how grand the house we build, if the foundations of our self are poor, our house will not stand for long.

Regardless of how big a game you wish to play in life or what legacy you choose to leave, when you find your life purpose – that thing that makes your heart sing – you find your passion and through it your true power.

Now that you have captured the first aspect of your life-purpose, The Gift of You, and wrapped it in an affirmation statement, it is time to work on the second aspect, the reflection, a compelling vision for your future.

A true 'life purpose' will always contain a vision to support you in achieving your prime purpose of being your best and giving your Gift. With your purpose as a guide, it is possible to discover your vision for your self by tracing the flow of your passion. The following exercise will help you to do so. The right brain, as well as being the passionate, emotional side, is also the side that has the power of vision.

Seven right-brain questions

These questions are designed to help you activate and access your right brain. It is important that you give the first answer that comes to you. Keep your answers short. Allow a maximum of thirty seconds on each question. It is essential to stay engaged with your right, feeling brain. The longer you analyse your answer, the greater the tendency to drift into your left, logical brain. Hence, trust the first intuitive answers that come to you and write them on a fresh page in your journal.

1. If you won a million pounds on the lottery what would you do differently in your life?

2. If your doctor told you that you will live in perfect health for another six months and then, without any suffering, will die, what would you do differently with your time?

3. What have you always wanted to do but have put off or maybe been afraid to attempt?

4. If I had a magic wand and could grant you one skill or ability, what would you choose?

5. What gives you the greatest feeling of pleasure and satisfaction in life?

6. What legacy do you want to leave; how do you want to be remembered?

7. What great dream would you dare to dream if you knew it were guaranteed to come true?

Once you have finished writing, look back at each answer and ask your self this question: 'Is my life and the way I am living it in alignment and harmony with my answers?'

The simple but fundamental truth behind this process is that nobody ever became great by doing something that they didn't enjoy. You can get by through doing something you don't enjoy, but you will never achieve true success and live your life to the full unless you are doing something that you love.

You don't need to go into detail or justify your answers – just be honest and clear with your self and give a simple 'yes' or 'no'.

Dare to Dream

Those who channel their passion into their work, making it their purpose, always achieve a greater result than those people who show up just for the money. In every area it is the people who are passionate about what they do and go the extra mile that make the biggest difference in life. This truth is so obvious that it begs the question, 'Why don't more people find a way to make their work their passion?'

While there are many varied answers to this, the most common one is that many people don't believe they could do it any differently. Often they have no sense of their passion and purpose or they lack the confidence to pursue them.

But once you begin to work on your *self* and raise your awareness, you will develop a genuine belief in your self and begin to trust your self and strive to realize your dreams.

The Veggie House Story

Whilst running a Goal Mapping workshop within a large company I was encouraging everyone to set goals and seek to make work their passion when suddenly one of the participants slammed down her pen, folded her arms and pulled a face that clearly said, 'I'm not playing!' I immediately asked her if she was OK, because up until that point she had seemed genuinely interested in the programme. Her response was quite intense: 'Its stupid and pointless. What's the use of getting myself all worked up about something I don't have and will never be able to afford?' I asked her what her dream was. Again her reply was somewhat negative: 'It's just a dream ... what's the use of allowing myself to hope when I'll just be setting myself up for disappointment?'

Reluctantly, almost through gritted teeth and with her arms still folded, she told me that her dream was to run a small vegetarian guesthouse up in the highlands of Scotland. After encouraging her to capture her dream and set it as a goal, she instantly retorted: 'But the reality is that I can't even afford the tiny one-bedroom flat I have now. What's the point of allowing myself to get distracted by daydreaming?'

After a little more encouragement she made a stand and took the step of *inwardly* declaring her belief in her self before she *outwardly* declared her vision by committing it to paper in the form of a Goal Map.

Three years passed before I met her again. As she began to tell me what had happened over that period her face lit up and she explained with excitement:

> To be honest, Brian, after your workshop I was a little irritated by you. I felt you had no right to make me get in touch with what I really wanted only to be faced with the realization of where I was and what I had. When I got home I told my partner all about my day and we both agreed that you were wrong.

> But then the strangest thing happened; a couple of days later, while looking through the paper, I spotted an advert for a small guest house for sale in the highlands of Scotland – a property that would be ideal for my dream. And while both my partner and I immediately dismissed it as 'only a dream', on about the third time that we turned back to that page for another look, the realization suddenly dawned. If we were really committed to this dream we could move in together, sell one of the flats (we each had one) and, with a little help from our parents, get together a deposit, arrange a mortgage and buy the place.

> Because it would take time to build up regular trade, we thought it would be foolish if both of us gave up work straightaway to run the guesthouse, so initially it was my partner who did this full time. Meanwhile, my company agreed to relocate me to Scotland.

> The past three years have flown by and I've never been happier. I've also produced some of my best work. But best of all, in another

couple of months I'm leaving to join my partner in running the guesthouse, because he's built up a great trade and is really busy.

It was great to hear how well things had turned out for her, but what really impressed me as she spoke was *who* she had become as a person. She was *being* a very different person from the one I had met three years earlier.

She had grown in and of her self. From taking the initial steps – raising her awareness, connecting with her passion and building her belief in her self – she had gradually engaged in an ever upward spiral of thought, feeling and behaviour. This had culminated in not only her physical goal (the guesthouse), but also, more importantly, the growth of her overall beingness as a person.

What's your dream?

Now review your answers to the seven right-brain questions. Connect with your passion and flow with it to imagine the physical activities that create it.

Give form to your vision by recording in your journal another affirmation statement, using ten words or fewer. As usual, write in the first person singular and the present tense and keep it positive.

You now have the two main ingredients for defining your life purpose – clarity about The Gift of You and clarity about your vision and passion. The remaining work is to identify the core synergy that unites and enhances them.

- - - - - - - - - - - - -

*Your life purpose may not be directly centred
on your work but you can always be
passionate about it, because your work is a
vehicle to help you live your purpose.*

- - - - - - - - - - - -

The Big Why

Sometimes people's life purpose revolves around what they do, sometimes it's more about who they are. Always, however, it will be connected to the difference they make. It is their big *why* – their ultimate reason for living – and fills their life with meaning.

Once, while talking with a group of sales people about going beyond motivation to a deeper level of compelling purpose, one of the delegates shared his story. 'First,' he said, 'I want you to understand that my purpose in life is not sales.' Several people were quite surprised at this announcement for he was one of the most successful people in the company. He went on to explain that his career in sales was the vehicle for achieving his purpose, which he felt was to provide the best possible start for his children.

I was a teacher, but I became disheartened with the system and the quality of education we give to children. I decided I wanted more than that for my own children; I wanted to give them a life education – take them places, show them something of the world, introduce them to other cultures and beliefs.

I knew that this would require considerable resources and would be almost impossible on my teacher's salary, so I started looking for some way to earn that sort of income. A friend of mine was doing really well in sales and I thought *If he can do it, so can I.* Of course, I wasn't any good at it at first; I didn't like it and was close to giving up and going back to teaching. But holding the awareness that I was doing it for my family gave me a sense of passion and power that I had never known before and gradually this helped me to move beyond any limitations and on to success.

This man was clear. He was clear about *what* he was doing, *why* he was doing it, *how much* he expected to receive each year for doing it, and for *how long* he would continue to do it. At the time he was about forty-two, already a wealthy man, and looking to slow down and take his family on a trip around the world.

Find your life purpose

- Find what it is that makes your heart sing – a compelling purpose that will act as a beacon for you to steer towards.

- Dare to dream. It is the first step on the path of conscious self-evolution.

- Exercise free will and work with your heart to live your prime purpose of being your best. Choose to become all that you can be – mentally, emotionally, physically, materially, socially and spiritually.

- Begin to complete this process now by creating a magical life purpose for your self and your life. Compose a 'portrait of purpose', combining the magnificent being that in truth you are with the magnificent life you desire to create for your self.

- Reconnect with the affirmations of your prime purpose – The Gift of You and your vision statement. Review your answers to the seven right-brain questions. Take full notice of your feelings and your passion. Most of all, sense your inner self and trust what comes up for you.

● Capture the essence of your life purpose by uniting The Gift of You and your vision for your future in one powerful statement of intent. Write this statement in your journal, keeping it short and to the point, using ten words or fewer.

For some people this process can take a little time before they are really clear. However, it is important to make a start because this in itself helps to bring clarity. You can then edit and reword as and when you are clear.

You may find it useful to remain aware of your prime purpose by each day asking your self the question, 'What is my life purpose?' Allow your subconscious genie to bring you the answer in its own time and in its own way. Be open, and listen.

Sow an act and you reap a habit.
Sow a habit and you reap a character.
Sow a character and you reap a destiny.

CHARLES READE

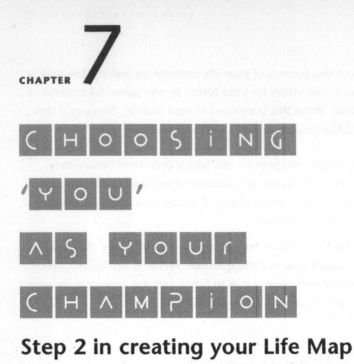

CHAPTER 7

CHOOSING 'YOU' AS YOUR CHAMPION

Step 2 in creating your Life Map

Once you make the fundamental choice to be the predominant creative force in your life, any approach you choose to take for your growth and development can work, and you will be especially attracted to those approaches which will work particularly well for you.

ROBERT FRITZ

Starting on Your Life Map

The journey we have travelled together through the pages of this book has so far followed a path that explores the guiding principles of creation and the dynamics of the human mind. From thought to belief and paradigm to purpose, the core message has focused on success being achieved through choosing to be your best.

The next step is to engage in the Life Mapping technique itself, so as to move beyond the awareness of your purpose and begin identifying and *mapping* the qualities of character that will support you in achieving it.

Your purpose will always be in some way *ongoing*; there will be ever greater insights, details and depths to be realized. However, the Life Mapping technique is designed to help you achieve whatever your current level of purpose is, even if this is simply to be your best you.

Once created, your Life Map quickly becomes a dominant focus for both 'the conscious you' and the 'subconscious you' to steer towards. It serves many roles – an anchor in stormy seas, a succinct reminder of your sincere desires, a filter for evaluating decisions. Your Life Map is like a signpost at the fork in the road; it points the way to your greatest good and supports you in making your best choices.

Make the investment in your self now! Take time to create your own Life Map. By building your self you empower every other aspect of your life. You are the source of your life. Nourish the source now and evolve your life through personal growth so that it thrives and blossoms.

Preparation

To create your Life Map there are several requirements that will help you achieve the best results. Perhaps the most important of these are an open mind and a willing heart.

Choose to create your Life Map from your best *way of being. Be* of good attitude. *Be* sincere in desire. *Be* committed to completing the process. Create your internal state.

There are also some things to do that are extremely beneficial:

- *Create and allocate quality time.* Ideally, two hours is great. However, in our workshops we complete the process in one hour or less. What is important is that you capture a snapshot, a succinct picture of your potential, and then enhance it over a period of time. You will see many benefits if you continue the process of working with your Life Map in the future. But make a start now, and for your first map allow a minimum of about an hour.

- *Create the space.* Find yourself a peaceful and inspiring location that reflects the desired internal space you wish to create. If the weather is suitable, it is great to do this type of creative exercise outside – in a park or garden for instance.

- *Create an ambiance.* If you are indoors you could put on some relaxing music and maybe burn some incense or light a symbolic candle. After all, it's not every day that you create a blueprint for your greatness.

. . . .

Treat the process as something of great value,
for it is, in fact, the process of valuing your self.

. . . .

Finally, here are some of the material things you need to create your Life Map:

- a set of coloured pens (colour is a powerful right-brain stimulant)
- a pencil, a pencil sharpener and a rubber
- a pen

- two sheets of A4-size (or larger) white paper or card (or your journal)
- a ruler
- an object about 45mm in diameter that you can use to draw circles around (for Template 2)

The Life Mapping technique uses two templates: one has seven boxes, the other seven circles, representing seven aspects or areas of life. Template 1 is focused for your left brain, Template 2 (see Chapter 8) for your right brain. When completed they produce a whole-brain Life Map mandala.

Left-Brain Words

First, copy Template 1 (overleaf) into your journal or on to a separate sheet of paper or card. Remember to mark each box with its quality.

Then, using your overall purpose statement from the end of the last chapter, or whatever you presently believe your purpose to be, write it as an affirmation in the central box marked 'Purpose'. (If you are still unsure of your overall life purpose use 'being my best me'. This will gradually help you to raise your awareness and clearly identify the other aspects for this step.)

It is important to construct your statement in the following way so that it has maximum impact on your subconscious.

- Keep it succinct, reduced to its essence – that's where the power is. Be definite and meaningful. Use as few words as possible – ten or fewer is best.
- Follow the *Three Ps of Power* by ensuring your statements are:

    personal (in the first person singular)

    in the *present* tense

    positively focused

For example, 'I am happy now' rather than 'I'm not sad anymore.'

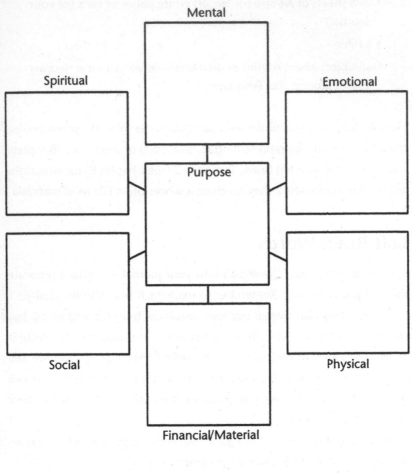

Mental

Spiritual

Emotional

Purpose

Social

Physical

Financial/Material

TEMPLATE 1

Often people in our seminars find it strange that we ask them to make a statement about something they want as if they already had it – stating that they feel on top of the world when in fact they don't. They reason and argue, 'I don't have this yet,' 'I don't actually feel that great', and therefore feel conditioned to start their statement with 'I want to …',

'I intend to ...', 'I am going to ...' The problem with this is that your subconscious mind doesn't understand time-lines in the same way that your conscious mind does. When you tell your self that your goal is in the future, your subconscious reads the literal picture and understands you to mean that it must keep this goal at arm's length.

If you use the three Ps to make your goals, intentions or commands – 'I want to be happy' – you will achieve that exact goal and 'want' to be happy. And each day thereafter you will achieve *wanting* to be happy.

To help stay in alignment with these principles try beginning your affirmation with the words 'I am ...'

- 'I am' – personal and in the present tense – commands power and magic.
- 'I am' carries the energy of belief and certainty.
- 'I am' creates a picture of you *being* your intention – a picture founded in the *now* – which is where your subconscious also operates.

Next, ensure your statement is focused on the positive – on what you *desire,* not what you dread – because, again, your subconscious obeys the literal picture. An example of a negative statement is 'I don't want to smoke any more.' You may know that your goal is to 'be free' of the habit, but the literal picture you give to your subconscious is one of you still smoking.

By seeing your self as you want to be and stating your intention as if it had already happened – 'I am free', 'I am happy', 'I am healthy', 'I am wealthy' – you command your subconscious genie into action and begin creating it as a reality.

In our workshops it's amazing how many people make a negative statement and describe what they don't want. Even after we have explained in detail why it's important to keep it positive, many people still fall into this trap.

Working out your purpose statement is an extremely thought-provoking process, and for some people it takes a little while before their statement has a satisfactory depth of meaning. Often we meet people from previous workshops who tell us how their purpose statement has evolved since they first created it. It took one company director two weeks of pondering before he eventually created a statement which he felt represented his life purpose. What he wrote on his initial map was 'I give all that I am in all that I do.' This was what started off his process of discovery. It is a very simple statement, but it had profound depths of meaning for the person who created it. For this man it meant that if he was in the office, then he was really in the office; if he was playing football, then he was really playing football; if he was at home with his family, then all of him was really at home with his family. He committed his self to living his life to the full and realized that one of the major aspects of achieving this was to be 100 per cent present and focused on whatever he chose to do.

Your purpose statement isn't written in stone. As you proceed on your journey of understanding your self, your clarity of purpose will naturally evolve, as will your statement.

When I first created the Life Mapping system I naturally decided to test it on my self first to discover its potential and how it could benefit my life. My original purpose statement read: 'I raise global awareness by becoming my best me.'

I thought very deeply about my self and what I believed my purpose and mission in life to be. The statement combines my chosen work and vision – 'helping as many people as possible to grow to new levels' – with my prime purpose of *being my best me* and leading by example.

I recently created a new map for my self, and although I have now produced many since my first one years ago, my central purpose has remained fundamentally constant – simply the detail of depth has become clearer.

My purpose statement is now: 'I am the light for transcendence.' My intention is the same as before, but the depth of my understanding has changed. I now *know* my purpose at another level – to be my highest self, to be an example for others who are seeking to transcend their self and arrive at greater levels of awareness and whole-life success.

Defining Your Champion

One of the most important foundations of the Life Mapping technique is understanding the following statement.

* * * * * * * * * * * *

The fundamental requirement for achieving your purpose is becoming the person who can achieve it.

* * * * * * * * * * * *

When you become the person who can achieve your purpose, the scenery of your life is created naturally, as a consequence (*effect*) of *who* you are consciously being at *cause*.

The next step of Life Mapping is to *choose* the best *ways of being* that will help you achieve your purpose. Choose the qualities which define *you as your champion* and *affirm* them by stating them in each of the six life areas on your template. Begin this process with the 'Mental' box at the top. Think again about your purpose, and at the same time, ask your self this question: 'Which one *mental* quality of character, when developed further, would serve me best in becoming the person who can achieve my purpose?'

Out of the many mental qualities – such as confidence, patience, commitment, positive focus – choose the first one that comes to you.

Trust that your subconscious is working with you and write the quality in a short, personal, positive and present-tense affirmation.

'Mental' examples:

- I am mentally free now.
- I am predominantly positive.
- I am patient.
- I am focused.

After writing your statement, move clockwise and ask your self the same question of the next box, 'Emotional': 'Which one *emotional* quality of character, when developed further, would serve me best in becoming the person who can achieve my purpose?'

Once again, consider your purpose and see your self having achieved it. Observe which qualities of your heart have empowered you most: love, passion, openness, compassion ...

As before, allow your self to be guided by your intuition and trust the first quality that comes to you. Then write it in the 'Emotional' box as an affirmation.

The same guidelines apply for each box, and the more that you work with your Life Map and ask 'Which quality would serve me best ...?', the greater levels of realization and clarity you will attain.

My original statement in the Emotional box was: 'I am heart centred in thought word and deed.' On my most recent map it has evolved to 'I live through my heart.'

'Emotional' examples:

- I open my heart to everyone I meet.
- I love and accept my self.
- I am compassionate.

Once you have created your statement move to the next box, 'Physical', and ask: 'Which one *physical* quality of character, when developed further, would serve me best in becoming the person who can achieve my purpose?' Focus on your overall wellbeing. Are you vibrant, energetic and active or are these some of the qualities that you wish to enhance or acquire?

My statement in the 'Physical' box is probably the one that has changed least over the years. Until my present map it was: 'I am positively vibrant with health and energy.' It is currently: 'I am balanced at all levels.'

'Physical' examples:

- I am healthy.
- I fulfil my physical potential now.
- I am full of boundless energy.
- I am alive and whole.

When you come to the 'Material' box, ask your self the question: 'Which one *material* quality of character, when developed further, would serve me best in becoming the person who can achieve my purpose?' Be mindful to give extra energy and focus to the *qualities of character* and *ways of being* that are most supportive in this area.

Many people lose their way a little here and state *doings* or *havings*, such as *'I do the work that I enjoy'* or *'I have enough money for my needs.'* Avoid these types of statements. They are more suited to goal setting with time-lines and progress steps. Life Mapping is about *being,* and most often a *being* statement will begin with the words 'I am'.

Even if your purpose involves the generation of material wealth, it will be your quality of character that creates it.

'Material' examples:

- I am abundant.
- I am prosperous.
- I am rich in mind body and spirit.
- I give and receive freely.

My own statement currently reads: 'I am the Master Magician.'

Once again, when you have created and written your 'Material' statement, move on to the next, 'Social'. Bear in mind here that the social aspect covers all relationships, including your relationship with your self. Ask: 'Which one *social* quality of character, when developed further, would serve me best in becoming the person who can achieve my purpose?'

The qualities that most often appear here are trust, honesty, openness and connection. Fundamental qualities such as these are universal and can apply to many different areas of your life at different times. Again, trust your 'gut feeling' and intuition to point out your path, which will naturally change and evolve to help you remain balanced as you grow.

'Social' examples:

- I bring out the best in other people.
- I love everyone.
- I am trusting and trust my self.
- I am open and sincere.

The final box in this process is 'Spiritual'. Often these qualities are the ones that people most want to acquire. Some that regularly appear in this box are faith, belief, fulfilment and contentment. Ask your self: 'Which one *spiritual* quality of character, when developed further, would serve me best in becoming the person who can achieve my purpose?'

Identify that quality now and write an affirmation statement for your spiritual aspect.

'Spiritual' examples:

- I believe in my self more each day.
- I am one with the universe.
- I am at peace with my self.
- I give my Gift freely.

Congratulations! You have just completed the first half of your Life Map, a set of balanced affirmations representing a blueprint or plan of *you* being your best – your chosen champion who can achieve your purpose.

CHAPTER 8

THE MANDALA OF LIFE

Step 3 in creating your Life Map

*Everyone can draw beautiful pictures; we do it every
day on the inside of our minds.
Bringing them to the outside brings forth the natural
artist in each one of us.*

BRIAN MAYNE

Preparing For Step 3

The power of Life Mapping does not come just from knowing about it or even understanding it in detail, but stems directly from taking action and engaging in it. It is the physical process and mental effort of creating your Life Map that produces the influence on your subconscious. Your next step generates the connection that produces the power.

On a fresh page in your journal – and I recommend the front or back page for easy revisiting – or on another sheet of paper or card, copy out Template 2 (overleaf) for your right brain.

If you use an object to draw around you will find, whatever its diameter, you can always fit six circles around the seventh or central one. The widest point of your completed mandala will be three times the size of your circular object, so make sure you have enough room around your central circle to draw one either side.

Place your first circle as near to the centre of your page as possible. Then draw the circles directly above and below, finishing with the two on either side. Drawing them in this order ensures that the position of your circles reflects the pattern of your left-brain template. And because it is a mirror image of that template there is no need to name the circles – simply leave them blank, as in the diagram.

Right-Brain Pictures

Your right brain is the major pathway to your subconscious and it thinks in pictures. So the next step is to turn your left-brain affirmations into right-brain visualizations. This part involves creating picture representations of your affirmation statements. To do this you can use symbols, line drawings or simple pictures. *Everyone can draw if they think 'I CAN'.*

I still remember clearly the resistance I felt towards drawing when I first began the techniques of Goal and Life Mapping. I felt a little timid

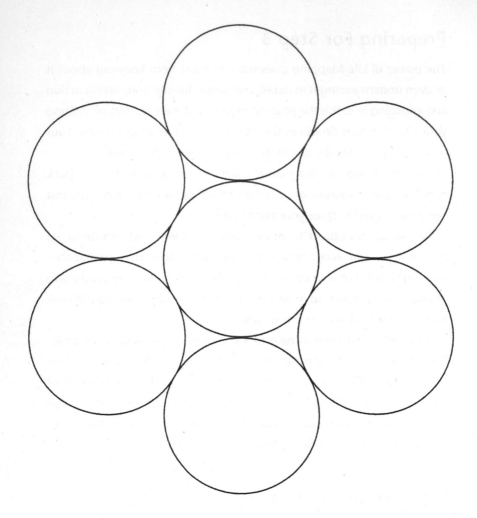

TEMPLATE 2

when I first ran the programmes in corporate workshops. And I could empathize with the people who said, 'I can't draw' or 'this is childish and unnecessary'. But more and more I realized that drawing was the real source of the power within the system.

If it has been a while since you did any drawing and the prospect seems daunting, then simply use stick men or symbols. You will find that once you get started your confidence will naturally grow, as will your enjoyment of this part of the process. Your right brain is your creative brain; once you begin exercising it by thinking in pictures it becomes *active* and thus brings you greater creativity and more ideas.

For some people the process of consciously thinking in pictures is difficult; they don't easily see how they can represent their written statements in a simple picture or symbol and are tempted to add words. But, again, it is the very process of concentrating on finding a picture that creates the depth of connection with and influence on your subconscious genie.

Above all else, the very best thing you can do for your self is *let it be fun*. Remind your self of what it was like when you were a child, free at heart, and give your self permission to be childlike again and play full out.

Many people find that this is the most enjoyable part of the process because they can express themselves in ways that they haven't indulged in for a long time, without any external judgement. In fact, no one else needs to be able to understand your drawing. This is a communication system between you and your subconscious genie. You are the only person who needs to know what your symbols or markings mean. No matter how simple they are, if these images have come from your mind your subconscious will understand them.

For example, one of my early affirmations in the 'Mental' area was 'I am free'. At first I had no idea how I could express this in a drawing, but the more I pondered the more ways I saw. Sometimes I found it very easy to *think* of a picture, but felt it would be very hard to draw it. My early attempts at drawing a 'blue bird of freedom, rising up on open wings' relied heavily on people's imagination! However, I knew what it meant, and the process of drawing it began to influence my subconscious. Not only that, but through repeating the Life Mapping process over a period of time, my ability to draw and express my self through pictures improved.

A turning point for me was using *symbols*. I discovered that I could extract the essence from a huge amount of meaning and attach it to a very simple symbol. Similarly, a cross and a swastika are both very simple drawings, no more than a few straight lines, but they each carry huge significance and meaning, which will vary slightly for different people.

The more I understood the power of symbols, the more I saw how to simplify my imagery. My picture of 'the blue bird of freedom' eventually became just two curved blue lines, but for me their meaning was as clear and as profound as my deepest thought.

For me, one of the biggest benefits to come from this process, outside of achieving my intentions, was learning to think in pictures and thereby rebalancing my brain. This helped me move to another level, where both my left-brain strategies and my right-brain creativity were much more effective.

One approach I've found to be very useful is to say your left-brain affirmation statement with feeling, and at the same time to close your eyes and observe whatever visual representation appears in your mind's eye. Once you have captured a picture that *feels* right, go on to consider how you could interpret it on paper.

Perhaps the best approach of all is just to *make a start* with the first picture that comes to mind, for whichever circle. Once you activate your creative right brain, other images and symbols will start to come to you. Below are four key things that will help you on this part of the process:

1   Use lashings of vibrant colour. Colour is a strong right-brain stimulant. The essence of the Life Mapping technique is to influence your subconscious. The more vivid you make your Life Map, the more power and connection you will achieve.

2   Put lots of physical effort into your drawings. The more effort you put in, the stronger the connection with your subconscious.

3   Move around and change your position to suit your self. You can create and change emotion through motion, so allow creative energy to flow through you by getting up and moving around whenever you feel the urge to.

4   HAVE FUN!

The examples given overleaf are those that have appeared most often in our workshops. While they may well inspire you, and you may even choose to adopt one or more for your own map, remember that you will always achieve your greatest power by coming up with your own images. Like the principles and qualities they are meant to represent, the examples below can be used in many or all of the various life areas.

Once you have drawn your visualizations in the six outer circles, place Templates 1 and 2 next to each other, side by side. Try switching them over to sense which way round feels right for you.

LIFE MAPPING PORTRAITS

LOVE

POSITIVE FOCUS

HAPPY

B-LEAF

COMET-MINT

A-BUN-DANCE

Life Map Examples

To give you an idea of how a Life Map comes together, on the following pages are three examples, together with their creators' affirmations and comments. Two of the Life Maps are reproduced in colour on the inside front and back pages of the book.

LIFE MAP FOR ANTON KORNBLUM

My Affirmations

Purpose: I lead and empower through 'bean' in creative action, now.

Mental: I remain focused and hold my vision.

Emotional: I open my self ever wider for ever deepening compassion.

Physical. I am vibrant with youth, strength, fitness and vitality.

Material/Financial: I embrace riches and prosperity in my life.

Social: I am fun 'tu-be' around.

Spiritual: I 'em'(Afrikaans for 'am') a vehicle for 'di-vine' expression.

This is my second Life Map. The first I did a year ago. Although I liked the first one it was quite intense, and intensity was the one part of my way of being that I wanted to change. This latest one, although a little corny, is light and makes me laugh. It's causing me to take myself lightly.

Equally importantly, I'm becoming the person I have affirmed and declared through the words and pictures. I'm experiencing myself more as a leader. Wealth – the part of my life that was most lacking – is now flowing more freely into my life. Possibly the area in which I've seen the greatest shift is the relationship with my wife, which is now more loving and compassionate than ever before.

In fact, all the areas are coming into fruition in a balanced way. Generally I feel more confident, more at ease and at peace with myself, and my usual optimism now seems to be underpinned by something a lot more solid and empowering than just optimism itself.

This system is simple yet very powerful. When I look at my map now, I no longer think of what the exact words are behind the pictures. I tend not to look at the individual pictures, but rather scan or have a 'swig' of the map as though it were a divine nectar. This brief daily 'taking in' of the Life Map seems to re-inform my consciousness at many levels, leaving me feeling tingly, humorous, positive and light hearted.

LIFE MAP FOR TINA SHAW
(See Tina's Life Map in colour on inside front cover.)

My Affirmations

Purpose: I am sharing and growing.

Mental: I believe in me.

Emotional: I am passionate.

Physical: I am dynamic.

Material/Financial: I am equal.

Social: I am truth and honesty.

Spiritual: I AM refuge.

When I started the Life Mapping process I was a little sceptical. How could this technique help me to know who I am and where my life fits? But, wow, through Life Mapping I am achieving my dreams and able to enjoy my challenges and treasure my relationships.

We all have dreams, but until you can capture the meaning of you they will never be attainable and never be goals. The seven circles of my Life Map show to everyone (and, above all, reveal to me) the essence of who I am, the sparkle and the magic that is me. This has made such a huge difference to my life it is hard to know how to put it into words.

If you are reading this and thinking 'So What?', then my advice is to give it a go. Why? Because if you don't you will never know how great you are!

LIFE MAP FOR VAL SCHUCH
(See Vals's Life Map in colour on inside back cover.)

My Affirmations

Purpose: I honour heaven on earth with all that I am.

Mental: I am wise, free and look for the gifts.

Emotional: I flow with my feelings and trust in my heart.

Physical: I am vital, balanced and full of life.

Material/Financial: I delight in the riches of life.
Social: I am love, connecting at core, sharing the dance.
Spiritual: I am pure love – in love with life.

My Life Map is a simple reminder of who I choose to be at my best. It reflects some of the core values and positive intentions in my life and gives me a balanced blueprint for all my different dimensions of being.

The more I focus on my Life Map the easier it becomes to be my best self. It is a clear visual representation for my subconscious. I have stuck it on the wall by my bed so I can see it regularly. Before doing something important, or if I feel I've lost sight of who I am or I feel knocked off balance, I conjure up the images of my Life Map in my mind and they help me feel centred again and hold me to being my best.

Looking back, the whole process of thinking about and creating my Life Map has helped me become clearer about who I am and who I choose to be. My map has changed and evolved over time, as have I. May you enjoy your map as much as I have mine.

9

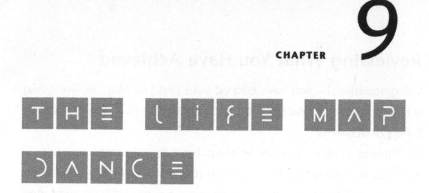

THE LIFE MAP DANCE

Living your Life Map

Dance as though no one is watching you,

Love as though you have never been hurt,

Sing as though no one can hear you,

Live as though heaven is on earth.

TRADITIONAL PRAYER

Reviewing What You Have Achieved

Congratulations! – you have created your first Life Map. Before going on to complete the final steps it is important to be clear about what you have just achieved.

Through creating your Life Map you have demonstrated your faith in your self by taking the first steps and forming a blueprint or plan for your future. You have given your genie your commands for the future YOU; you have created the beginnings of a new *dominant* or steering thought. Give your self credit for this important achievement.

Throughout this book, the base principle of the information and ideas we have shared is:

. . . .

You create your own reality.

. . . .

For richer or poorer, better or worse, happy or sad, *you,* just like every-one else in the world, are creating, influencing and shaping your experience of life, and you achieve this primarily through the thoughts that you think. Remember, each thought that you think begins a cycle of creation. The thoughts you hold most often and feel most strongly become targets for your genie and are a preview of some of your life's forthcoming attractions.

. . . .

Through your focus you have the power to choose which thoughts you wish to make dominant.

. . . .

One of the keys to success is to hold your focus on what you want. While this principle is simple and clear, the majority of people find it relatively difficult to hold their focus on their chosen desires. Instead, their self is preoccupied with the fears, worries, habits and many distractions of life. This often results in the creation of the very opposite of what they desire in their heart because, like it or not, we create what we spend most of our time looking at.

At best this diminishes our power, often resulting in two steps forward and one step back, and at worst it leads to massive self-sabotage and makes what we feared a reality.

Learning to focus and hold your thoughts to create your desired results is a universal skill; it applies equally to long-term vision and momentary events. However, even on a comparatively short time-scale, many people find it difficult to maintain concentrated focus on their intentions.

For example, if I were to ask you to meditate on the thoughts and images that represent you being 'your best you', and think intensely about only that for, say, a minimum of thirty minutes in order to create a new dominant thought, I expect you would find it is not an easy task. Most people, including myself, would too. It may sound simple, but in reality we become distracted by something or start to ache or fidget, and sometimes we get bored, become sleepy, our mind drifts and our focus wanders. Learning to hold our focus is an art to be mastered.

However, this is exactly what you have just achieved in creating your Life Map. For the period of time it took you to do this, you held your focus. The physical process means that for each image you drew on your Life Map you also created a mirror image in your mind and, therefore, the beginnings of new dominant thoughts. It is the very act of creating your Life Map – the physical effort of putting pen to paper and the mental focus on visual symbols – that creates the deep connection with and influence on your subconscious.

Increasing the Power

A large degree of the power generated through Life Mapping is achieved because it works on many different levels simultaneously. At an unconscious level your Life Map operates in the manner that has been previously outlined – as a target for your subconscious genie to aim for. At another level it succinctly captures and represents the insights you have had and the choices you have made. It is therefore a conscious reminder of what you have chosen as your greatest or *highest good*.

In this way your Life Map is a condensed blueprint for your potential and you can hold it up as a conscious guide or filter for your thoughts when making decisions. Regardless of the detail, situation or terrain, your Life Map operates like your personal 'true north' – it will always point to your chosen best or highest good. It will be a constant and stable core in a fast-changing and uncertain environment. Remember, your Life Map has been tailored by you personally and it is focused on you being your best. By navigating your life towards it, and by it, you will ultimately achieve your best results.

At whichever level you choose to focus, your Life Map is an aid to support you in achieving that most precious of all human gifts – conscious self-evolution. The ability to choose to be your best you is the ultimate goal in life; the greatest of all successes is being able to be at your best on an ongoing basis.

It is now important that you continue to build on the power of the connection you have already made with your genie. The pulls and pressures of life can be strong and cause many to drift from their intentions unless they remain mindful.

Even though in the moment that we make resolutions and commitments we feel clear and strong, afterwards influences and challenges can wear us down so that our mental and emotional state drops, our low self rises to become more dominant, our paradigm changes and we have a tendency to see everything through a filter of ego or a mask of doom and gloom. It is like being in a fog. We forget our insights and promises to our self or others and are instead drawn towards our conditioning and habits. It requires earnest intention, energy and focus to shift and surpass old ways of being or ingrained habits and paradigms.

Work with your Life Map by focusing on it for a few moments each day and you will be able to hold your awareness for longer, override self-doubt and gradually strengthen your influence on your subconscious genie.

The remainder of this chapter is dedicated to some of the additional steps you can take to enhance your Life Map, your self and your life. Together they form a 'support system' to help you achieve your purpose, become your best you and fully live your Life Map. Each step covered builds on the previous work and helps strengthen the power of your dominant thought and thus raise the level of your self.

You can choose to engage in these extra steps at any time in the future or straight after creating your Life Map. The choice is entirely yours; however, I strongly recommend that you take the first one immediately.

Step 1 – Make a Commitment

The first step in living your Life Map is to make a commitment to it. Do this by placing your signature on your map and making a heartfelt promise to keep your word to your self. This is what a signature really stands for, your word.

George Zaluki, an American speaker and author, quotes one of my favourite definitions of commitment. He states: 'True commitment is doing the thing that you said you would do, long after the mood in which you said it in has left you.'

Many of us make momentary commitments to our self and others. When say we are going to do something, in that moment we usually mean it, but often after a while our mood changes and we don't feel the same. Our motivation wanes and our commitment ceases to be a priority or is forgotten altogether.

True commitment is about claiming your power by keeping your word to your self. Each time you keep your word you increase your power. Each time you keep your word to your self and do the thing that you said you would do, you raise the level of your self-esteem, feel stronger and are in a better position to keep your word in the future.

The ability to keep our word to our self is part of the foundations from which every truly successful person has grown. Practise first on the small things in life – by keeping your word on everyday occurrences – and you will develop the habit of commitment and make it easier to keep your word on the bigger things.

It would be naive to go to the gym only once and expect to be fit. Exercise has to be an ongoing activity if we wish to remain healthy. In the same way, influencing your subconscious to steer towards success and consciously choosing to be your best are ongoing practices and lifelong pursuits.

Commitment itself is an ongoing and active process, not an individual event. It involves making a choice in any given moment and continuing to make choices as and when necessary in order to keep the commitment.

* * * * * * * * * * * *

Commitments are the equivalent of the choices we make in each moment.

* * * * * * * * * * * *

THE LIFE MAP DANCE

The technique of Life Mapping is designed to make it easier to keep your commitment by working with your subconscious. However, everything is governed by the universal principle that *What you give you receive*. In some way, what you put in determines what you get back out. It is good to really stretch your self every now and again. Choose to be your best. If it helps, choose one day at a time. Choose a quality of greatness to live by each day and gradually build your commitment muscle by exercising your free will.

Step 2 – Share and Prosper

For this step I would like you to make another commitment – to share the essence and key points of Life Mapping, as you understand them, with at least one other person (a friend, colleague or family member, perhaps) at some time over the next two or three days.

When you share this information with another, both of you receive a gift. You are helping not only someone else but also your self. A fundamental shift takes place in your own attitudes and paradigms when you see your self as the teacher as well as the student. More than this, when you stretch to explain something to someone else, you often discover some deeper understanding. Plus, by teaching this information you are repeating it and committing it to your long-term memory. This results in strengthening your command to your own subconscious genie, thereby building greater belief in your self and your abilities.

Step 3 – Put Up the Picture

As we travel through life it is almost inevitable that we will experience periods of light and dark, pleasure and pain, happiness and sorrow. There will be times of self-doubt, negativity and fear. Like the currents of the ocean, these can, if left unattended, pull us from our chosen course. But by looking at your Life Map once a day you will be able to regain your bearings. Just a few moments each day of concentrated focus will help dispel any lingering negativity and remind your subconscious of your intended purpose and chosen qualities.

By restating aloud your affirmations and repicturing your visualizations, you can progressively condition your Life Map mandala to grow in power and thereby become the target for your subconscious to steer towards.

I strongly recommend that once you have completed your Life Map you place it somewhere highly visible so it acts as a conscious reminder. One of my favourite spots is my bedroom wall, where I can see it just before I sleep at night and when I wake in the morning.

Some people choose to place their Life Maps around the house as action motivators. Children often take them to school and put them up in class. And many people scan them on to their computers and use them as screen savers.

The most effective times of day to connect with your Life Map are first thing in the morning and last thing at night. Your brain operates at different frequencies and rhythms throughout a twenty-four-hour period and these are the times when your brain is naturally in the alpha (daydream) state, when the connection with your subconscious can be up to a hundred times greater. Just a few moments invested in your self at these prime times can therefore bring a massive reward to all areas of your life.

In whichever way you choose to use your Life Map to remain conscious of your greatest good, make a commitment now to look at it at least once a day for the next thirteen days. This period of time should be long enough for the establishment of new habit patterns.

Step 4 – Live Your Life Map

The higher you raise your awareness, the greater your conscious ability to create your reality. The better you genuinely know your self, the greater your ability to choose to be at your best. And the more that you understand of the processes of creation, the more harmoniously you can work with the current of life and flow towards your intentions.

Awareness is akin to wisdom – it is a product of both experience and study, a deep *knowing* that is drawn from the combination of being and doing. One of the major keys to increasing your wisdom and achieving success is to capture your insights and remind your self of important lessons.

One of the most powerful tools for personal growth – and something that has helped me enormously – is writing down my thoughts in a journal. When I first came into contact with personal development I started the practice as a way of holding the ideas, pieces of wisdom and insights I was gleaming, and to remember the lessons I had learned. Over the years I have now filled several books with these thoughts, and I find it extremely valuable to reread them every so often and ensure that the lessons are remembered and employed.

I have also discovered that journal writing in combination with Life Mapping is extremely powerful and helps to take it to another level.

Once each day for thirteen days, I capture in my journal my experience of living my Life Map, a process which deepens the connection to my subconscious genie. Each process becomes an anchor for the other – my Life Map encourages me to regularly use my journal and my journal helps me to capture the wisdom reflected from my Life Map.

Journal writing is a great way to reflect on your self. Create the time to write about your innermost thoughts, feelings, beliefs and experiences – you will find it truly rewarding and enlightening.

The Optimum Process

Through much research, personal experience and testing, Sangeeta and I have found the following to be the optimum *supercharged* process for accelerating growth through Life Mapping. The approach focuses on living your Life Map in harmony with BE–DO–HAVE to the fullest degree.

The process involves a powerful thirteen-day cycle of conscious intention and commitment that will result in real breakthroughs of enlightenment and abundance. It is best started on the first day after completing your Life Map.

Supercharge your Life Map

Step 1

I recommend that you make a colour photocopy of your Life Map, reduced in size so that it will fit on a page of your journal. Next, carefully cut around the outside of your mandala and paste it into either the front or back of your journal or on to a plain piece of paper or card.

Step 2

Over the next six days work around the outer circles of your mandala, starting at 'Mental' on day one and finishing with 'Spiritual' on day six. Using your journal, identify the doings – specific actions and behaviours – that would best serve and support you to live fully the quality or beingness for that area. For example, if your 'Mental' affirmation is 'I am positively focused', your key behaviour could be to make all your conversation positive, thereby helping you to build a positive outlook.

Writing in your journal will help you explore and identify the actions or behaviours that will best support the achievement of your chosen quality or way of being. For instance, on my most recent map, 'balance' is my physical quality. When I used my journal to reflect on what balance actually meant to me and how I could enhance it, it became increasingly obvious that more regular physical activity and exercise would be of great benefit. I quickly identified not only a number of different ways in which I avoid exercising – by making excuses and justifications – but also new and deeper reasons for pushing on and actions that I could take on a regular basis to support my chosen way of being.

At the end of each day, once you are clear on which action or 'doing' offers most support for the quality or way of being you are working on, draw a symbol or picture of it just to the side of that 'beingness circle' and attach it with a little wavy line (see example overleaf). As you work around your mandala, ask your self questions in order to identify and draw your most supportive action or doing.

Step 3

After the first six days you will have a set of entries in your journal and six symbols or pictures representing your chosen actions around the outside of your mandala. The process now continues for another six days, going round the mandala once again but this time using your journal to identify the having for your doing.

Choose a milestone or an inspiring goal for your actions to aim for. Again, each day identify and draw an image or symbol to represent your desired having. Place your goals either next to or above your doing picture, and once again connect them to your doing with a wavy line.

We are all a combination of be, do and have. By raising your awareness of who you choose to be, things that you can do and

A LIFE MAP WITH ADDITIONAL PICTURES

rewards you wish to have, and committing your self to follow through with what you have learned, you live within the natural be–do–have syntax of success and set in motion a powerful and progressive upwards spiral. It takes only a few moments at the end of your day, but sends a powerful command to your subconscious genie.

Step 4

On the thirteenth day focus your energies on the centre circle of 'Purpose' and your overall map. This day is about completion and contemplation of the whole and your experience over the period. It is also about self-acknowledgement and celebration for achieving one full cycle of thirteen days.

Use your journal on this day to capture the many blessings that the last twelve days have afforded you, and recommit your self for another thirteen if this feels right. You can either continue with your existing map and dedicate your self to living it fully for another period of thirteen days, or use the insights from your journal to create a new Life Map.

Finally, identify the perfect gift you will give your self – a token or gesture that reflects a genuine 'pat on the back' and a celebration of your purpose and greatness.

Goal Mapping

For the achievement of more complex goals, use Goal Mapping, a sister technique of Life Mapping. The Goal Mapping system follows the same universal principles and utilizes the same process of drawing symbols for right-brain activation, but its focus is predominantly on *having and doing*, or goals and actions. Unlike Life Mapping, this system encompasses a time-line and *how, who* and *when* steps that will lead you to your goals. (See Resources, page 204, for more details.)

When used together, Life Mapping and Goal Mapping form a comprehensive platform of be–do–have which helps you define and map in great detail any aspect, area or desire so that you can enrich your life. The combination thus offers Maximum Sensory Stimulation.

Maximum subconscious influence is achieved through maximum sensory stimulation and repetition. The three prime senses are sight, sound and touch (visual, auditory and kinaesthetic). Most of us use a mixture of all three but have a preference for one.

You will achieve a certain level of influence with your subconscious by visualizing your map, a higher level by also stating your affirmations aloud, and an even greater level by creating physical sensations in your body.

Choose to play full out, either for a day or a thirteen-day period, by picturing your Life Map symbols for your right brain while stating your affirmations for your left brain and simultaneously physically stepping into 'character' and being your chosen quality.

Either first thing in the morning, or at any time through the day when you genuinely desire to give your best, turn on the full power of your Life Map by symbolically stepping into it and becoming it. Make it part of your self by consciously choosing to feel, and physically step into an imagined circle containing your quality at the same time as you visualize and affirm it.

Life Mapping for Your Higher Guidance

An inherent 'intuitive intelligence' is woven into the very fabric of life. Everything at some level appears to know its purpose, what it is doing. Nature tells itself how to be. This self-organizing system extends from a micro subatomic level (where two particles separated by a relatively great distance maintain a connection in some way and a change in one triggers a change in the other) through a macro level (where all the billions of different cells in the human body choose to work together to create the synergy of a person) to all the different plants and animals that are inter-dependent on each other and make up ecosystems and worlds, solar systems and galaxies.

. . . .

A web of intuitive, self-organizing intelligence permeates everything, and each and every one of us can consciously learn to tune in to it.

. . . .

I always marvel at how my dog intuitively knows to eat certain types of grass if his body lacks minerals. I'm amazed at how shoals of fish or flocks of birds, sometimes numbering thousands, can change direction instantly and in total harmony. I'm amazed at research showing that plants not only know when someone is in their space but can also sense that person's emotions.

The latest theories and findings from science confirm what ancient wisdom and teachers have always maintained – that at a deep level *everything is connected to everything else.*

At a subatomic level the particles that make atoms are not themselves made of matter but are fluctuations of intelligence and energy. You and I, every-one and every-thing, are all made of atoms, which are in turn made of particles, or energy and intelligence. Once, we were all just stardust and starlight at the centre of a sun. We are all, at our deepest levels, fluctuations of intelligence and energy rising up from a universal field. Each person is connected to this field of intelligence and energy in the same way that each individual wave is connected to the ocean. We spring from it, we exist as we travel our path, and eventually we return to our source.

In animals, guidance by this universal intelligence is called instinct. In humans we know it as intuition. Our minds are like the interface that tunes into this 'super highway' of collective consciousness and allows us to flow with the current of life towards our chosen purpose and goals.

The Field

I recently watched a great film called *The Legend of Bagger Vance*. The story centres on the relationship between an American golfer and his caddy in the 1930s. The caddy (played by Will Smith) coaches the golfer (Matt Damon) to *find the field*. By working with his mind the golfer connects with a deeper level of awareness and gets to *know* the right line and power for his swing and thereby plays his best game and goes on to victory.

We can all find the 'Field' in some way or another, whether it be in relation to sport, business, art or simply dancing. When you allow your self to just *be*, you set your self free. You can then tune into your essence, connect with the Field, and flow with the current.

Experiencing your awareness shift and tuning in to the Field is part of the journey of life. At some point most people will experience naturally flowing with the moment and achieving something complex with an effortless grace. Likewise, having a hunch or intuition which was not at all logical but which turned out to be perfectly correct is also an experience of being connected to the Field.

Many people ignore this sense, often because they have been schooled that it is not to be trusted, let alone acted upon. However, the further you travel through life and follow your intuition, the more you will come to trust its accuracy. Even top-level executives that I work with are taught that *after applying all of their left-brain evaluation criteria, they should check in with their intuition or 'gut feeling' and go with that.*

To connect with the Field you must become one with it. Be aligned and attuned to it. *Be it.* Remember, the Field is *all*, which means that you are already part of it and are, therefore, also *all*.

Think back to Chapter 1 on paradigms and the list of 'magic moment' positive qualities that are frequently cited. The reason so many different people define similar qualities around magical moments is because they are identifying some of the *prime qualities of the Field itself*. When you experience a magical moment you are in the flow and current of life. You are plugged into the Field and are therefore at one with it. By *being* or living the qualities of the Field, you align with it, tune in to it and merge with it.

Now choose some of the qualities of your magical moments as the qualities for a Life Map. They will most likely be in alignment with the qualities of the Field. If you then live your Life Map and be those qualities, you become the Field. Experience it for your self. Choose to really *be* the qualities of your magical moments and notice the difference it brings to your day.

Tune In To the Rhythm

Freedom is one of the core qualities of the Field, and of existence. Regardless of the detail, when you consciously connect with the Field you are invariably *free* in your self, free from your own judgements or habitual paradigms. Practise *being* as mentally free as a child at play, free from preconceived limitation and conventions. You will quickly connect with your essence and discover the bliss of living your True Self.

The Bliss of True Self

This ancient truth of the human spirit can be found in the wisdom literature of virtually all cultures. One of the most inspiring and classic examples that I have discovered is the Gospel of Thomas.

You will not find this gospel or much reference to it in any of the bibles for it was condemned as heresy and burnt by the church in the third century AD. It was thought that all copies had been lost until one was discovered in a clay jar in the deserts of Egypt in 1947 and fragments of another in an ancient library. It has now been translated and is an original, unaltered first-century record of the teachings of Jesus.

The Gospel of Thomas comprises many short statements which gradually build to form a higher and higher understanding or state of awareness. It is only a short book but, being the words of a master, is succinct and multidimensional in its wisdom. Each time I read it I discover something new and my paradigm shifts.

Throughout the book there are references to heaven as 'The Kingdom', and what I find particularly interesting, and probably one of the main reasons why it was burnt, is that it says you don't need the church or a priest to find this Kingdom. It states, 'The Kingdom is within you and all around you.' It also offers guidance on how to enter the Kingdom; the essence of the instruction is to quieten your small self, or ego, and focus on your True Self – your High Self, your best you.

The Gospel of Thomas repeatedly uses an important word to describe this process of entering the Kingdom or connecting to your High Self – *metanoia*. The word comes from ancient Greek and literally means *a change in your knowing* or, in more modern terms, a paradigm shift.

My paradigm shift when I first came into contact with the book was realizing that heaven is not so much a place as a *way of being,* and that therefore I have the power to choose to live my whole life there.

A New Perspective

We are now back where we began our journey together – shifting paradigms. Only now perhaps you are seeing the same territory anew, from a different perspective and a higher state of being.

Sangeeta and I would like to thank you, our friends, for journeying with us. Allow us once more to remind you that you have the power to create magic in your life; you have the power to choose your *way of being.* Choose those *ways of being* that are in harmony with entering the Kingdom or the Field.

Simply by choosing to *be* your best, you will in some way be choosing the qualities of the Field – naturally and automatically. By reaching for your own authentic greatness, by *being your best you*, you will invariably connect with your essence and discover the Kingdom for your self.

Sow Simple

There is much information in this book. However, at heart, the philosophy covered is very simple:

- Be your best YOU and you will naturally create your best life.
- Think your very best thoughts and you will trigger your best feelings which will influence your best actions and effectively create your best results.

Each thought is a seed. Simply sow the seeds that will grow into the best you. Think your best about your self, your situations and other people, and you will naturally begin to create a magnificent and magical life.

As a final thought and inspiration, consider this: if enough of us stretch to be our best, then together we will naturally create a little more of the heaven that is right here on earth just waiting to be embraced.

Look Well To This Day

Look well to this day, for it is life, the very best of life.
In its brief course lay all the realities and truths
of existence – The joys of growth, the splendour
of action, the glory of power.
For yesterday is but a memory, and tomorrow
is only a vision.
But today, if well lived, makes every yesterday
a memory of happiness, and every tomorrow
a vision of hope.
Look well to this day.

FOUND ON A CLAY TABLET IN THE RUINS OF BABYLON

A CONCISE GUIDE TO LIFE MAPPING

The fast track to creating your Life Map

We are what we repeatedly do.

Excellence then is not an act, but a habit.

ARISTOTLE

Before You Begin

This appendix has been designed to assist those people who have read the main part of the book and now wish to create another Life Map.

Live Your Life According to the Fundamental Principles of Creation

1 Direct life changes towards your desires

In this rapidly changing world, learning how to direct the changes towards your desires is the key to success.

Think about the recent changes you have experienced.

What was your attitude towards them? Did you build windmills or walls?

2 Create change in your self by shifting your paradigm

Your paradigms are the filters through which you see life and the blueprints used by your subconscious to select your behaviour. When your paradigm changes, so do you.

When you look at your self what do you see?

Describe your self, including what you say to your self and how you genuinely feel about your self.

Are your attitudes and behaviours in alignment with your paradigm?

Is your paradigm the one you desire? If not, rewrite it.

3 Fine tune your beliefs

Your beliefs are the tap that turns your potential on or off. Whatever you believe to be true for you, *will* be true. By fine-tuning your beliefs you bring your paradigm of life into focus.

Are your current beliefs in alignment with your preferred paradigm?

If not, rewrite your Beliefs Grid (page 47).

4 Review your beliefs

Whether you believe you can or can't do something, you're right. Limiting beliefs = *I can't*. Empowering beliefs = *I can*. Ask your self:

Where did this belief come from?

Whose idea was it, mine or someone else's?

What caused me to decide that this was true for me?

In what ways have I changed since forming this belief?

Does it still serve me?

Think about which beliefs will help you move forwards in life and rewrite your old belief in a more empowering way.

5 Become fully 'response-able'

You are *able* to *choose* your *response* and determine your own path. It is your ultimate freedom. Reconsider your beliefs and responses by repeating the Response-ability exercise on page 77.

6 Create your reality

Your life is created and shaped through your thoughts. Becoming 'response-able' in your thinking allows you to steer your life and access your true power.

Repeat these words regularly: *If it's to be, it's up to me.*

7 Move towards your focus

Whatever you focus on grows in your awareness. By choosing your focus wisely you enhance your self. Think back over the last few days and ask your self:

What has my dominant focus been on – what I want or what I don't want, what I desire or what I dread?

8 Think your best thoughts and create your best life

Each of your thoughts triggers a cycle of emotion, attitude, behaviour and action leading to results. So, think the thought, feel the feeling, influence the action. You become what you think about – your dominant thought.

Check if your dominant thought is focused on what you like or don't like about your self.

Check your focus on other people. Are you focusing on their merits or failings?

View your current situations. Are you focusing on what is going right or wrong?

9 Understand that who you are 'being' makes the biggest difference.

Being is the power behind *doing* and results in *having*. Your right brain is the source of your *being,* your left brain the source of your *doing*. When these two sides are balanced you can create your desires, or *having,* and develop any *way of being* or quality at will.

What are your core qualities or ways of being?

10 Be a human 'being', not a human doing

We are human *beings* first and foremost. Work with the natural flow of evolution by giving *being* priority over *doing* and *having*.

What are my intentions and desires?

Who do I need to be to create my desires?

What do I need to do to create my desires?

11 Make being your true self your prime purpose

Your prime purpose is to give The Gift of You by being your best.

Write a statement that best describes The Gift of You.

What is unique and special about you?

What do people admire most about you?
What do you love most about your self?
What do you enjoy most about your self?
If you cannot see your gift, repeat the exercise on page 134.

12 Define your goals in life

We have an innate need to seek a sense of meaning and purpose in life. Your goals support your prime purpose of being your best and allow you to give The Gift of You. Redefine your vision by answering the Seven Questions on page 143.

13 Build peace in your self and create peace in the world

Self-discovery is unending. Think thoughts that will create experiences of peace, happiness and abundance.

Create Your Life Map

Ensure you create your Life Map from your best *way of being*.

Step 1

Prepare your left- and right-brain templates (see pages 154 and 164).

Step 2

Identify your current balance and which life areas you need to enhance. Give your self a score of between 1 and 10 in each of the following areas. Be intuitive and honest, and listen for the first number that comes to you.

Mental ... .   Emotional ... .   Physical ... .

Financial ... .   Social ... .   Spiritual ... .

Now plot your scores on to the wheel below, starting from the top spoke (Mental) and moving round clockwise. Then link the numbers you have ringed, like a dot-to-dot puzzle. This will give you a picture of your current sense of balance.

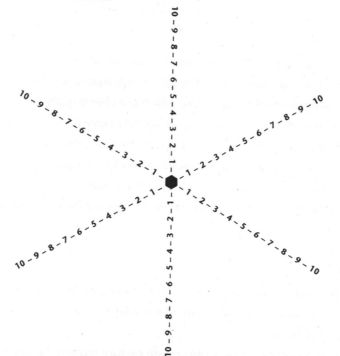

The aim is to have an even circle, though most people have a dip or two. This is not a negative sign but simply indicates where you need to put your focus and energy in order to bring your self back into balance and thus become more effective in all your pursuits in life.

Step 3

Recheck your life purpose affirmation statement. Do you still believe it represents The Gift of You and your vision for your life? If you have become aware of new insights, create a new statement or amend your existing one to bring it into alignment with your current paradigm. Use ten words or fewer, and keep it *personal, positive* and in the *present* tense. Write your statement in the central box of your left-brain template (page 154).

Step 4

Choose your ways of being and affirm them in each of the six life areas on your mandala, starting with 'Mental'. Think again about your purpose while asking your self this question: *Which one mental quality of character, when further developed in my self, would best serve me in becoming the person who can fulfil my purpose?* Choose the first quality that comes to mind. Trust that your subconscious is working with you and write the quality in a personal, positive and present-tense affirmation statement. Once again, keep it to ten words or fewer. Then repeat for the other five areas.

Step 5

Turn your left-brain affirmations into right-brain visualizations. The major pathway to your subconscious mind is through your right-brain, which thinks in pictures.

Using Template 2 (page 164) create picture representations of your affirmation statements, using symbols, line drawings or simple images.

Many people find it useful to state aloud with feeling their left-brain affirmations and close their eyes to see what visual representation appears in their mind's eye.

Use lashings of vibrant colour to stimulate your right brain. The more vivid you make your Life Map, the more powerful the connection.

Put lots of physical effort into your drawings so as to have maximum impact on your subconscious.

Move around and allow creative energy to flow through you.

Put Templates 1 and 2 next to each other and begin drawing your additional visual representations (see example on page 186).

Step 6

As a mark of your commitment, sign your Life Map. As you do so, make a heartfelt promise to keep your word to your self.

Step 7

Share the essence and key points of Life Mapping with at least one other person to gain a deeper connection with your self.

Step 8

Place your Life Map so it will be a reminder to your genie just before you go to sleep at night and when you wake in the morning.

Invest a few moments each day for thirteen days to review your Life Map. By restating aloud your affirmations and repicturing your visualizations you progressively condition your Life Map mandala to grow in power and become the target for your subconscious to steer towards.

resources

LIFT International was founded by Brian and Sangeeta Mayne.
We are a community of Light leaders. We give Life Information For Transcendence in order to serve the evolution of humanity.

LIFT International products and services available include:

Goal Mapping – The System for Success (a comprehensive study pack with six audio tapes)
The most successful men and women have been those who have learned to develop the natural mental ability of goal setting. The Goal Mapping system has been specifically designed to do this by powerfully impressing your subconscious mind on your consciously chosen goals. Goal Mapping is without doubt the most powerful system for goal achievement in any area of life.

Goal Mapping Surfers' Guide
An easy to use guidebook walking you through the key steps to creating your Goal Map. This handbook also features individual accounts and Goal Maps to inspire and encourage you to create the life of your dreams. ISBN 0-9533161-4-9

Goal Mapping Live (audio cassette)
A 65-minute inspirational overview of the power of positive focus and the system of Goal Mapping. ISBN 0-9533161-0-6

Goal Mapping Pack (audio cassette)
Six audio tapes (running time approximately 4 hrs 30 min) and a 50-page workbook with practical exercises, examples and illustrations. ISBN 0-9533161-1-4

Forthcoming titles:

Sam the Magic Genie

Sam the Magic Genie is a truly enchanting story about a small boy who embarks on an insightful adventure with his magic genie, Sam. Together they explore the vibrant world of choice and thought – discovering how our thoughts produce our feelings, which in turn shape the life we create for ourselves. ISBN 0 09 188945-6

Joseph's Journal

A companion booklet to Sam the Magic Genie, designed to assist children in understanding and creating their own Goal Maps. ISBN 0-9533161-5-7

For information about:

• any of the above products

• attending Life Mapping, Goal Mapping or Personal Leadership workshops

• keynote addresses to organizations

• LIFT's coaching services

contact LIFT International
Tel: +44 (0)1264 782543
www.liftinternational.com
enquiries@liftinternational.com

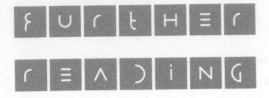

Further Reading

Buzan, Toni, *The Mind Map Book: how to use radiant thinking to maximise your brain's potential*, Plume Books, 1996

Cameron, Julia, *The Artist's Way*, Putnam, 2002

Coelho, Paulo, *The Alchemist*, HarperCollins, 1999

Covey, Stephen, *The Seven Habits of Highly Effective People*, Simon & Schuster, 1999

Frankl, Victor, *Man's Search For Meaning*, Beacon Press, 2000

Hay, Louise, *The Power Is Within You*, Eden Grove, 1991

Johnson, Spencer, *Who Moved My Cheese?*, Vermillion, 2002

Maltz, Maxwell, *Psycho Cybernetics*, Simon & Schuster, 1960

Oakley, Ed, and Doug Krug, *Enlightened Leadership: getting to the heart of change*, Simon & Schuster, 1994

Patent, Arnold M, *You Can Have It All*, Gill & Macmillan, 1996

Ross, Hugh McGregor, *The Gospel of Thomas*, Watkins, 2002

Walsch, Neale Donald, *Conversations With God*, Hodder Mobius, 1997

Whitworth, Laura, Henry Kimsey-House, Phil Sandahl, *Co-Active Coaching*, Davis-Black, 1999

Zukav, Gary, *The Seat of the Soul*, Rider, 1991